THE MARBURG GROUP'S COMMENTS ON THE EUROPEAN COMMISSION'S PARENTHOOD PROPOSAL

AF776033

An open access version of this book is also available online, thanks to funding from LMU Open Access Fonds.

THE MARBURG GROUP'S COMMENTS ON THE EUROPEAN COMMISSION'S PARENTHOOD PROPOSAL

Christine Budzikiewicz
Konrad Duden
Anatol Dutta
Tobias Helms
Claudia Mayer

INTERSENTIA
Cambridge – Antwerp – Chicago

Intersentia Ltd
8 Wellington Mews
Wellington Street | Cambridge
CB1 1HW | United Kingdom
Tel: +44 1223 736 170
Email: contact@larcier-intersentia.com
www.larcier-intersentia.com

Distribution for the UK and
Rest of the World (incl. Eastern Europe)
NBN International
1 Deltic Avenue, Rooksley
Milton Keynes MK13 8LD
United Kingdom
Tel: +44 1752 202 301 | Fax: +44 1752 202 331
Email: orders@nbninternational.com

Distribution for Europe
Lefebvre Sarrut Belgium NV
Hoogstraat 139/6
1000 Brussels
Belgium
Tel: +32 (0)2 548 07 13
Email: contact@larcier-intersentia.com

Distribution for the USA and Canada
Independent Publishers Group
Order Department
814 North Franklin Street
Chicago, IL 60610
USA
Tel: +1 800 888 4741 (toll free) | Fax: +1 312 337 5985
Email: orders@ipgbook.com

The Marburg Group's Comments on the European Commission's Parenthood Proposal
© Christine Budzikiewicz, Konrad Duden, Anatol Dutta, Tobias Helms, Claudia Mayer 2024

The authors have asserted the right under the Copyright, Designs and Patents Act 1988, to be identified as authors of this work.

An online version of this work is published under a Creative Commons Open Access license (CC-BYNC-ND 4.0), which permits re-use, distribution and reproduction in any medium for non-commercial purposes, providing appropriate credit to the original work is given. If you create a derivative work by remixing, transforming or building upon the material, you may not distribute this without permission. To view a copy of this license, visit https://creativecommons.org/licenses/by-nc-nd/4.0/.

Intersentia was granted an exclusive commercial license to print and distribute the printed version of the book.

Enquiries concerning reproduction which may not be covered by the Creative Commons Open Access license above should be addressed to Intersentia.

All versions of this work may contain content reproduced under license from third parties. Permission to reproduce this third-party content must be obtained from these third parties directly.

Artwork on Cover: 'Bauhaus Stairway', Oskar Schlemmer (1888–1943). Digital image, The Museum of Modern Art, New York/Scala, Florence.

ISBN 978-1-83970-513-7
D/2024/7849/79
NUR 820

British Library Cataloguing in Publication Data. A catalogue record for this book is available from the British Library.

PREFACE

This volume documents the Marburg Group's comments on the Parenthood Proposal of the European Commission (COM(2022) 695 final of 7 December 2022); the comments were first published online on 10 May 2023 (www.marburg-group.de) and in a short version in a German private international law journal (IPRax 2023, 425). The comments are the product of several group meetings held between December 2022 and May 2023. They have been linguistically reviewed and complemented by occasional references to more recent contributions dealing with the Parenthood Proposal. The legislative resolution of the European Parliament on the Parenthood Proposal (P9_TA(2023) 0481 of 14 December 2023) could not be considered in these comments.

We thank Heike Speier and Maureen Koets (both Marburg) for their invaluable help in tackling the editorial challenges of this group publication.

Marburg, Leipzig, Munich and Regensburg, February 2024

Christine Budzikiewicz, Konrad Duden, Anatol Dutta, Tobias Helms and Claudia Mayer

CONTENTS

Introduction

The Parenthood Proposal

1) On 7 December 2022, the European Commission published a Proposal for a Council Regulation on jurisdiction, applicable law, recognition of decisions and acceptance of authentic instruments in matters of parenthood and on the creation of a European Certificate of Parenthood[1] (in the following: the Parenthood Proposal, PP).

2) The Commission proposes, for the area of parenthood – defined as the 'determination in law of the relationship between a child and each parent' (Art. 4(3) PP) – common rules for the Member States addressing the classic issues of private international law: jurisdiction in parenthood matters (Art. 6 et seq. PP), the applicable law to parenthood (Art. 16 et seq. PP) and the recognition of court decisions in parenthood matters (Art. 24 et seq. PP). Furthermore, inspired by the European Certificate of Succession, the Commission recommends the introduction of a European Certificate of Parenthood enabling European citizens to prove a parenthood position throughout the European Union with uniform effects (Art. 46 et seq. PP). Finally, the Parenthood Proposal targets the cross-border circulation of authentic instruments on parenthood with two separate regimes: not only shall the evidentiary effects of authentic instruments be extended to other Member States (Art. 44 and 45 PP), as already under the Succession Regulation (Regulation (EU) 650/2012 of 4 July 2012 on jurisdiction, applicable law, recognition and enforcement of decisions and acceptance and enforcement of authentic instruments in matters of succession and on the creation of a European Certificate of Succession [2012] OJ L201/107). Following the concepts of the Brussels IIb Regulation (Council Regulation (EU) 2019/1111 of 25 June 2019 on jurisdiction, the recognition and enforcement of decisions in matrimonial matters and the matters of parental responsibility, and on international child abduction [2019] OJ L178/1), the Commission also suggests that authentic instruments with binding legal effects shall be recognised (Art. 35 et seq. PP).

The need for common rules

3) The Group welcomes the initiative of the Commission. A European Regulation on parenthood in cross-border cases would close a gap in the existing private

[1] COM(2022) 695 final.

international law acquis of the European Union. The existing instruments – in particular, the Brussels IIb Regulation, the Hague Child Protection Convention, the Maintenance Regulation (Council Regulation (EC) 4/2009 of 18 December 2008 on jurisdiction, applicable law, recognition and enforcement of decisions and cooperation in matters relating to maintenance obligations [2009] OJ L7/1), the Hague Maintenance Protocol and the Succession Regulation – only deal with the legal consequences of parenthood (parental responsibility, maintenance and succession upon death), but not with the preliminary question of legal parenthood itself. Against this background, creating a framework for harmonious decisions by common rules on the recognition of parenthood within the European Union would enhance the efficiency of these other instruments and would, thus, be a valuable contribution to the area of freedom, security and justice. Additionally, the existing conflict rules of the Member States on parenthood differ considerably,[2] creating disharmonies between the European legal systems. Currently, as to the parenthood of one and the same person, different substantive laws can apply, leading to irreconcilable statuses. Further complexity is added to the subject by recent case law of the Court of Justice of the European Union (CJEU), in particular, its *Pancharevo* decision. Here the Court of Justice established a duty of the Member States to recognise a parenthood status, *in concreto* the co-motherhood of the mother's wife under Spanish law.[3] The exact boundaries of this duty to recognise are far from clear. These uncertainties for European citizens in cross-border parenthood cases could be reduced by uniform rules, in particular, on the law applicable to the establishment and termination of parenthood.

4) The Group recognises the political obstacles for a European instrument on parenthood, bearing in mind that a future Regulation on parenthood would have to be adopted unanimously by the Member States in the Council, after consulting the European Parliament, in accordance with Art. 81(3) of the Treaty on the Functioning of the European Union. The Parenthood Proposal touches on controversial issues such as surrogacy and same-sex parenthood, as well as the status of biological parents if legal parenthood is attributed to social parents. Hence, it is doubtful whether unanimity in the Council will be attained or whether a Regulation on parenthood can only be realised with limited effects by enhanced cooperation between some Member States under Art. 326 et seq. of the Treaty.

---

[2] See, for example, the country reports in *Duden/Dutta/Helms/Mayer*, 'Eltern in ganz Europa – das Internationale Abstammungsrecht in Deutschland, Frankreich, den Niederlanden, Polen und der Schweiz', Frankfurt am Main 2023.

[3] CJEU 14 December 2021, Case C-490/20 (*V.M.A. v. Stolichna obshtina, rayon 'Pancharevo'*), ECLI:EU:C:2021:1008.

5) The Group appreciates the efforts of the Commission in drafting the Parenthood Proposal. Developing uniform private international law rules in the area of parenthood is rather challenging, not only, as already mentioned, because of the vast differences in the Member States' laws, but also because there are no existing models for common rules which could give guidance. This is unlike the area of succession upon death and matrimonial property (the subject of the last private international law projects), which the European legislator concluded through the Succession Regulation and the Property Regulations for spouses and registered partners (Council Regulation (EU) 2016/1103 implementing enhanced cooperation in the area of jurisdiction, applicable law and the recognition and enforcement of decisions in matters of matrimonial property regimes [2016] OJ L183/1 and Council Regulation (EU) 2016/1104 implementing enhanced cooperation in the area of jurisdiction, applicable law and the recognition and enforcement of decisions in matters of the property consequences of registered partnerships [2016] OJ L183/30). Here, the legislator could at least partly rely on previous work achieved by other institutions. Common rules on international parenthood have to be drafted mainly from scratch. In particular, the Hague Conference on Private International Law has, so far,[4] not addressed parenthood. The International Commission on Civil Status has not adopted comprehensive conventions in this field, either, but has rather addressed only some issues in older conventions.[5]

Deficiencies of the Parenthood Proposal

6) Although the Group embraces the initiative and the overall structure of the Parenthood Proposal, it suggests some fundamental changes apart from technical amendments, which are also documented in these comments. Some of the rules proposed by the Commission would create considerable problems in practice and could even lead to confusion. The European legislator should keep in mind that issues of parenthood are dealt with in most Member States on a daily basis by civil status officers with no university education in law, unlike in the other areas of private international law covered by the EU acquis, where mainly judges and lawyers are involved. Hence, there is a particular need for clear rules that can be easily applied in daily practice. Furthermore, the Group has the general impression that the Commission often simply copied solutions from previous instruments, in particular, the Succession Regulation and the

[4] See, however, the project of the Hague Conference on parentage and surrogacy, for details: www.hcch.net/en/projects/legislative-projects/parentage-surrogacy (last accessed 15 January 2024).

[5] For example, in the Rome Convention of 14 September 1961 extending the competence of authorities empowered to receive declarations acknowledging natural children and the Brussels Convention of 12 September 1962 on the establishment of maternal descent of natural children.

Brussels IIb Regulation, without considering the substantive and procedural particularities in the area of parenthood.

7) During the discussions in the Group – which took place in several meetings between December 2022 and May 2023 – the following main deficiencies of the Parenthood Proposal have been identified:

- Regarding **jurisdiction** (see below para. 28 et seq.), the Group welcomes, in principle, that **Art. 6 PP** offers a variety of general jurisdictional bases in order to facilitate the clarification of the child's parenthood. Certain jurisdictional bases therein, however, appear to be exorbitant and should be restricted. In Art. 6 PP, this concern relates to the jurisdiction based on the habitual residence or nationality of either parent and to the jurisdiction at the place of birth of the child (Art. 6(d) to (f) PP). Additionally, the provisions in **Art. 7 to 9 PP** that are intended to protect the child from a lack of jurisdiction through a jurisdiction based on the presence of the child, the recourse to national law and a *forum necessitates*, are too broad and should be amended. To compensate for these restrictions, the Group proposes a new jurisdictional basis in **Art. 6(aa) PP** at the simple residence of the child, which is, however, only available if the habitual residence of the child cannot be determined. This proposed rule can more specifically address the goals pursued by the provisions which the Group suggests restricting.

- In respect to the **coordination of proceedings** (see below para. 52 et seq.), the rule on *lis pendens* in **Art. 14 PP** should be adapted – both in relation to the scope of application and the legal consequences of a stay of proceedings – in order to address the fact that decisions in parenthood matters under national law often have *erga omnes* effect, because they relate to a status relationship.

- Regarding the rules on **applicable law**, the Group welcomes **Art. 17(1) PP** as a good starting point. This provision bases the applicable law on the habitual residence of the person giving birth at the time of birth, since a child has a strong connection to the birth mother, and it is easier to determine the habitual residence of an adult than that of a newborn child. However, it would not be appropriate to further apply the law of the State of the habitual residence of the birth mother for an indeterminate period of time after birth, although mother and child might have moved to another country or the child might have been separated from the birth mother (for example, in cases of surrogate motherhood). Therefore, after the initial allocation of parenthood at birth, the applicable law should no longer be determined by the mother's habitual residence at the time of birth but by the child's habitual residence – as proposed by the new Art. 17(2) PP (see below para. 65 et seq.).

- The Group also welcomes, in principle, that **Art. 17(2) PP** offers a set of alternative connecting factors in order to avoid the application of a discriminatory national law. However, the scope of this rule is far too wide, and it covers, at closer look, a number of cases for which it was clearly not intended and where it creates unwanted complications and uncertainties. The underlying favouring tendency should be maintained, but the provision should be tailored more precisely to cases where it is really necessary to provide alternative connecting factors in order to avoid the application of a discriminatory national law (see below para. 67 et seq.).

- Art. 4(3) PP indicates that the term 'establishment of parenthood', which is used in Art. 17 PP, also covers the contestation of parenthood. It would be more transparent, however, to expressly spell out in a **new Art. 17a PP** that the law applicable to the termination of parenthood is, in principle, the law under which parenthood was established. Additionally, it should also be possible to resort to the law of the State of the habitual residence of the child at the time of termination of parenthood (see below para. 83 et seq.).

- Art. 3(2)(e) PP excludes intercountry **adoptions** in the sense of the Hague Adoption Convention from the scope of the proposed Regulation. This exclusion does not mean, however, that all adoptions that fall within the scope of the Parenthood Proposal are purely domestic adoptions and never raise questions of international jurisdiction or applicable law. For those adoptions which do not fulfil the criteria of the Hague Adoption Convention but contain, nevertheless, an international element, the applicable law should be specified in a **new Art. 18a PP**. The main connecting factor in this context should be the *lex fori* of the Member State in which an adoption is pronounced (see below para. 98 et seq.).

- Since the provisions on **recognition of decisions** in **Art. 24 to 32 PP** essentially correspond to the acquis in already existing EU Regulations, the Parenthood Proposal is, in principle, based on a functioning and proven system of recognition of decisions. However, with regard to the grounds for refusal of recognition (Art. 31 PP), the Parenthood Proposal inappropriately takes over provisions that have been introduced mainly in the area of parental responsibility (Art. 39 of the Brussels IIb Regulation). While these specific provisions in Art. 39 of the Brussels IIb Regulation consider the special requirements in the area of parental responsibility, according to which the circumstances for the decision may change over time, status decisions on parenthood are largely based on static aspects. This is, *inter alia*, why the considerations in Art. 39 of the Brussels IIb Regulation cannot be transferred as the grounds for refusing recognition in parenthood cases. Among other things, the Group therefore calls on the European legislator to thoroughly revise the grounds for refusing recognition (see below para. 122 et seq.).

- The Group is of the opinion that there is no room and no need for a special recognition regime for **authentic instruments with binding legal effect,** such as proposed by the Commission in **Art. 35 to 39 PP**. Rather, the provisions on the recognition of court decisions in Art. 24 et seq. PP and on the acceptance of authentic instruments in Art. 44 et seq. PP suffice and should not be weakened by another set of rules. The Group has significant doubts that the types of instruments that could potentially be encompassed by the provisions proposed in Art. 35 et seq. PP exist at all in the current laws of the Member States. Rather, the legal effects of private declarations contained in an authentic instrument set up in one Member State are already 'recognised' by the other Member States, based on the duty to apply the law governing the establishment of parenthood under Art. 16 et seq. PP. Hence, the Group strongly advocates that Art. 35 to 39 PP should be deleted (see below para. 143 et seq.).
- Although the Group endorses the approach of the Commission in **Art. 44 and 45 PP** to extend the **evidentiary effects of authentic instruments** to other Member States, it proposes some adjustments to the civil status particularities of authentic instruments certifying parenthood (see below para. 161 et seq.).
- The Group is of the opinion that there is no need for the introduction of a **European Certificate of Parenthood** such as proposed by the Commission in **Art. 46 to 57 PP** (below para. 178 et seq.). Doubts about the necessity of such a Certificate arise primarily from the fact that the effects of the Certificate are limited to the presumptions set out in Art. 53(2) PP and the effect according to Art. 53(3) PP. Assuming that the presumption according to Art. 53(2) PP is a rebuttable presumption, the Certificate ultimately has no advantages over the recognition of court decisions and authentic instruments with binding legal effect (Art. 24 to 43 PP) and, at most, marginal advantages over the acceptance of authentic instruments with no binding legal effect (Art. 44 and 45 PP). As far as Art. 53(3) PP is concerned, the provision would only have an independent significance if the registration of parenthood is required for acquiring or establishing rights based on parenthood. Such cases appear to be rather rare. In the Group's view, an authority should be able to refuse to register parenthood in its relevant register if the recording would conflict with the legal situation in the Member State concerned (see below para. 207).

- Irrespective of the recommendation not to introduce a European Certificate of Parenthood, **Art. 46 to 57 PP** show some inconsistencies that call for a detailed revision (see below para. 176 et seq.).

- The Group proposes to make some adjustments to the **transitional provisions** in **Art. 69 PP** (see below para. 217 et seq.). The proposed amendments mainly concern the intertemporal application of the provisions in Chapters III and VI. The aim is to avoid legal uncertainties in transitional cases.

8) The Group mainly focused on the text of the proposed provisions and did not systematically review the Recitals, which have to be adjusted accordingly. However, the Group noticed that the Recitals partly do not match with the proposed Articles. Furthermore, the Annexes need a thorough review and better coordination with the procedural and substantive rules on parenthood in the Member States; otherwise, practical problems could arise (see below para. 171 et seq.). Finally, a careful editing of the different language versions of the Parenthood Proposal seems necessary. While the Group has mainly focused on the English text, a cursory reading of the German language version revealed many inconsistencies (see, for example, below para. 199).

CHAPTER I **SUBJECT MATTER, SCOPE AND DEFINITIONS**	**~~SUBJECT MATTER,~~SCOPE AND DEFINITIONS**
Article 1 **Subject matter**	**~~Article 1~~** **~~Subject matter~~**
This Regulation lays down common rules on jurisdiction and applicable law for the establishment of parenthood in a Member State in cross-border situations; common rules for the recognition or, as the case may be, acceptance in a Member State of court decisions on parenthood given, and authentic instruments on parenthood drawn up or registered, in another Member State; and creates a European Certificate of Parenthood.	~~This Regulation lays down common rules on jurisdiction and applicable law for the establishment of parenthood in a Member State in cross-border situations; common rules for the recognition or, as the case may be, acceptance in a Member State of court decisions on parenthood given, and authentic instruments on parenthood drawn up or registered, in another Member State; and creates a European Certificate of Parenthood.~~

Comments

9) The Group proposes to delete Art. 1 PP, which only repeats the official title of the future Regulation. The other private international law Regulations adopted so far by the European legislator do not contain a comparable provision. The scope of the future Regulation is already comprehensively defined in Art. 3 PP. Art. 1 PP, if kept in the present form, could, thus, create confusion.

Article 2 **Relationship with other provisions of Union law**	**~~Article 2~~***Article 65a*
1. This Regulation shall not affect the rights that a child derives from Union law, in particular the rights that a child enjoys under Union law on free movement, including Directive 2004/38/EC. In particular, this Regulation shall not affect the limitations relating to the use of public policy as a justification to refuse the recognition of parenthood where,	1. This Regulation shall not affect the rights that a child derives from Union law, in particular the rights that a child enjoys under Union law on free movement, including Directive 2004/38/EC. ~~In particular, this Regulation shall not affect the limitations relating to the use of public policy as a justification to refuse the recognition of parenthood where,~~

under Union law on free movement, Member States are obliged to recognise a document establishing a parent-child relationship issued by the authorities of another Member State for the purposes of rights derived from Union law.	~~under Union law on free movement, Member States are obliged to recognise a document establishing a parent-child relationship issued by the authorities of another Member State for the purposes of rights derived from Union law.~~
2. This Regulation shall not affect Regulation (EU) 2016/1191, in particular as regards public documents, as defined in that Regulation, on birth, parenthood and adoption.	

Comments

10) Art. 2 PP deals with the relationship of the future Regulation with primary and secondary EU law.

Relocation of Art. 2 PP to the general and final provisions (Chapter IX)

11) The Group proposes a relocation of this provision to Chapter IX. It is very unusual to clarify the relationship with other provisions of the law of the European Union at the beginning of a Regulation. Following the example of Art. 76 of the Succession Regulation, Art. 2 PP belongs to the general and final provisions dealt with in Chapter IX of the Parenthood Proposal.

No need to clarify the precedence of primary EU law

12) Furthermore, the second sentence of paragraph 1 should be deleted. It is self-evident that primary EU law takes precedence over secondary EU law, such as the future Parenthood Regulation. Moreover, such a provision would be a novelty in the private international law Regulations. So far, any interpretation of (primary) EU law by the Court of Justice of the European Union[6] was not codified in the Regulations. The reference in sentence 1 to primary and secondary EU law, conversely, can be justified by the close interconnectedness between free movement and issues of parenthood.

[6] Here in CJEU 14 December 2021, Case C-490/20 (*V.M.A. v. Stolichna obshtina, rayon 'Pancharevo'*), ECLI:EU:C:2021:1008.

Article 3 **Scope**	
1. This Regulation shall apply to civil matters of parenthood in cross-border situations.	
2. This Regulation shall not apply to:	
(a) the existence, validity or recognition of a marriage or of a relationship deemed by the law applicable to such relationship to have comparable effects, such as a registered partnership;	
(b) parental responsibility matters;	
(c) the legal capacity of natural persons;	
(d) emancipation;	
(e) intercountry adoption;	(e) intercountry adoption *within the meaning of the 1993 Hague Convention on Protection of Children and Cooperation in Respect of Intercountry Adoption*;
(f) maintenance obligations;	
(g) trusts or succession;	
(h) nationality;	
(i) the legal requirements for the recording of parenthood in a register of a Member State, and the effects of recording or failing to record parenthood in a register of a Member State.	
3. This Regulation shall not apply to the recognition of court decisions establishing parenthood given in a third State, or to the recognition or, as the case may be, acceptance of authentic instruments establishing or proving parenthood drawn up or registered in a third State.	~~3. This Regulation shall not apply to the recognition of court decisions establishing parenthood given in a third State, or to the recognition or, as the case may be, acceptance of authentic instruments establishing or proving parenthood drawn up or registered in a third State.~~

Comments

13) Art. 3 PP describes – using the established technique of prior EU instruments on private international law – the scope of the future Regulation. The Group advocates two minor amendments.

Exclusion and definition of intercountry adoption (Art. 3(1)(e) PP)

14) By 'intercountry adoption' the Parenthood Proposal refers – according to Recital 27 – to an intercountry adoption within the meaning of the 1993 Hague Convention on Protection of Children and Cooperation in Respect of Intercountry Adoption. This definition of the term 'intercountry adoption' is not self-evident; it therefore would be preferable to clarify this aspect in the Regulation itself. For further details on conflict rules for adoptions, see below para. 98 et seq.

Art. 3(3) PP redundant

15) Art. 3(3) PP is redundant, since its content already follows from the recognition provisions, which only apply to decisions on parenthood given in a Member State. Moreover, the current instruments of the European Union for the recognition of decisions do not contain a comparable provision.

Article 4
Definitions

For the purposes of this Regulation, the following definitions apply:

1. 'parenthood' means the parent-child relationship established in law. It includes the legal status of being the child of a particular parent or parents;

2. 'child' means a person of any age whose parenthood is to be established, recognised or proved;

2. 'child' means a person of any age whose parenthood is to be established, recognised, proved *or terminated*;

3. 'establishment of parenthood' means the determination in law of the relationship between a child and each parent, including the establishment of parenthood following a claim contesting a parenthood established previously;

	3a. 'termination of parenthood' means the dissolution of the legal parent-child relationship;
4. 'court' means an authority in a Member State that exercises judicial functions in matters of parenthood;	4. 'court' means ~~an authority in a Member State that exercises judicial functions in matters of parenthood~~ *any judicial authority and all other authorities of a Member State with jurisdiction in matters of parenthood which exercise judicial functions or act pursuant to a delegation of power by a judicial authority or act under the control of a judicial authority, provided that such other authorities offer guarantees with regard to impartiality and the right of all parties to be heard and provided that their decisions under the law of the Member State in which they operate,* *(a) may be made the subject of an appeal to or review by a judicial authority; and* *(b) have a similar force and effect as a decision of a judicial authority on the same matter.* *The exercise of judicial functions requires that the authority is generally entitled to adjudicate disputes between the parties.*
5. 'court decision' means a decision of a court of a Member State, including a decree, order or judgment, concerning matters of parenthood;	
6. 'authentic instrument' means a document that has been formally drawn up or registered as an authentic instrument in any Member State in matters of parenthood and the authenticity of which:	

(a) relates to the signature and the content of the instrument; and

(b) has been established by a public authority or other authority empowered for that purpose by the Member State of origin;

7. 'Member State of origin' means the Member State in which the court decision on parenthood has been given, the authentic instrument on parenthood has been formally drawn up or registered, or the European Certificate of Parenthood has been issued;

8. 'decentralised IT system' means an IT system as defined in point (4) of Article 2 of [the Digitalisation Regulation];

9. 'European electronic access point' means an interoperable access point as defined in point (5) of Article 2 of [the Digitalisation Regulation].

Comments

16) Art. 4 PP contains the usual list of definitions and follows the technique also used in the other private international law Regulations.

Termination of parenthood, Art. 4(2) and (3a) PP

17) The scope of the Parenthood Proposal not only covers the establishment but also the termination of parenthood. However, the Commission in its proposal, clarifies this only rather indirectly when Art. 4(3) PP refers to the 'establishment of parenthood following a claim contesting a parenthood established previously', cf. also Recital 33 in sentence 2.

18) Against this background, it should be made clearer that proceedings, decisions and authentic instruments concerning the termination of parenthood

(such as paternity contestations or challenges) are also covered by the planned Regulation. The termination of parenthood can also be a first and necessary step in another person's ability to assume the parental position (for example, by judicial determination or private declarations, see also below para. 87).

More precise definition of court, Art. 4(4) PP

19) The definition of the term 'court' in Art. 4(4) PP only requires that the authority in a Member State exercises judicial functions in matters of parenthood but does not specify what is meant by 'judicial functions'.

20) The Group is of the opinion that the definition of the term 'court' requires a more precise description by the European legislator, especially in order to achieve a clear delimitation of the areas of application of Chapters II and IV on the one hand, and Chapter V on the other hand. In more recent European Regulations, the European legislator already uses a more detailed definition. The wording in the Parenthood Proposal falls behind this standard. This deviation should be corrected, especially in light of the recent CJEU case law in *TB* (Case C-646/20; see below para. 22 et seq.). The proposed amendments are based on Art. 3(2) of the Succession Regulation (cf. also Art. 3(2) of the Property Regulations for spouses and registered partners; Art. 2(2) of the Maintenance Regulation) but add another clarifying sentence with regard to the 'exercise of judicial functions'.

21) It should be clear from the outset that civil status authorities issuing civil status documents (such as birth certificates or excerpts from the civil status register) are not 'courts' within the meaning of the Parenthood Proposal. Neither the receipt nor the registration of an acknowledgment of paternity makes a civil status authority a 'court'. Accordingly, they are not bound by the jurisdiction rules in Art. 6 et seq. PP. Public documents issued by civil status officers are not recognised as court decisions under Art. 24 et seq. PP, but fall within the scope of Art. 44 and 45 PP. This exclusion of civil status authorities is, however, not sufficiently clear from the wording of the definition in Art. 4(4) PP. The fact that, from the point of view of the European legislator, not every authority that is competent in matters of parenthood under national law is a 'court' also becomes evident in the indirect reference to Art. 6 et seq. PP in Art. 48 PP: the authority issuing a European Certificate of Parenthood does not need to have jurisdiction under Chapter II, but only needs to be the authority of a Member State whose courts have jurisdiction.

22) A precise definition of the term 'court' became particularly relevant and urgent with the recent CJEU decision in the *TB* case,[7] in which the Grand

[7] CJEU 15 November 2022, Case C-646/20 (*Senatsverwaltung für Inneres und Sport, Standesamtsaufsicht v. TB*), ECLI:EU:C:2022:879; see annotions by *Dutta*, Zeitschrift für das

Chamber changed long-standing case law.[8] In terms of content, the Court of Justice had to deal with an Italian private divorce with the participation of a registrar and had to clarify whether it is a judicial decision within the meaning of Art. 21 of the Brussels IIa Regulation (Council Regulation (EC) 2201/2003 of 27 November 2003 concerning jurisdiction and the recognition and enforcement of judgments in matrimonial matters and the matters of parental responsibility [2003] OJ L338/1) or an authentic instrument or party agreement within the meaning of Art. 46 of the Brussels IIa Regulation. The CJEU is of the opinion that the Italian private divorce before the registrar is a 'judgment … pronounced by a court of a Member State' within the meaning of Art. 2(4) of the Brussels IIa Regulation, which is consequently to be automatically recognised in all Member States pursuant to Art. 21 of the Brussels IIa Regulation. Prior to *TB*, the CJEU held – particularly in the context of the European Succession Regulation – that an authority is a court or exercises judicial functions only if that type of authority can, at least in principle, decide cases on a contentious basis, even if the case in question was of a non-contentious nature.[9]

23) *TB* creates uncertainty about the definition of the term 'court' across different Regulations.[10] While the CJEU, at the beginning of *TB*, emphasises the importance of the uniform application of Union law across different legal acts,[11] the substantive decision in *TB* deviates considerably from the definition established by the CJEU case law so far.[12] In *TB*, the Grand Chamber ruled with regard to the comparable definitions of the term 'court' in Art. 2(1) of the Brussels IIa Regulation (Art. 2(2)(1) of the Brussels IIb Regulation) and of the term 'judgment' in Art. 2(4) of the Brussels IIa Regulation (Art. 2(1) of the Brussels IIb Regulation). The Court of Justice stated that it would be:

> apparent from that definition given in the Brussels IIa Regulation itself that … that regulation is capable of covering divorces which have been

gesamte Familienrecht 2023, 16; *Gruber*, Zeitschrift für das Standesamtswesen, Familienrecht, Staatsangehörigkeitsrecht, Personenstandsrecht, internationales Privatrecht des In- und Auslands 2023, 2; *Löhnig*, Neue Zeitschrift für Familienrecht 2023, 119; *Mayer*, Zeitschrift für Europäisches Privatrecht 2023, 455.

[8] cf. hereto *Mayer*, Zeitschrift für Europäisches Privatrecht 2023, 455.

[9] CJEU 16 July 2020, Case C-80/19 (*EE*), ECLI:EU:C:2020:569, para. 51; CJEU 23 May 2019, Case C-658/17 (*WB v. Notariusz Przemysława Bac*), ECLI:EU:C:2019:444, para. 55 and 56; CJEU 21 June 2018, Case C-20/17 (*Vincent Pierre Oberle*), ECLI:EU:C:2018:485, para. 43, 44 and 56.

[10] CJEU 15 November 2022, Case C-646/20 (*Senatsverwaltung für Inneres und Sport, Standesamtsaufsicht v. TB*), ECLI:EU:C:2022:879, para. 39 et seq.

[11] CJEU 15 November 2022, Case C-646/20 (*Senatsverwaltung für Inneres und Sport, Standesamtsaufsicht v. TB*), ECLI:EU:C:2022:879, para. 40.

[12] See quotes, above n. 9.

> granted at the end of both judicial and extrajudicial proceedings, provided that the law of the Member States also confers jurisdiction in relation to divorce on extrajudicial authorities.[13]

According to the CJEU:

> [t]he EU legislature ... made it clear, with a view to ensuring continuity, that divorce agreements, which have been approved by a judicial or extrajudicial authority following a substantive examination carried out in accordance with national laws and procedures, constitute 'judgments' within the meaning of Article 2(4) of the Brussels IIa Regulation and of the provisions of the Brussels IIb Regulation which replaced it, and that it is precisely that substantive examination which distinguishes those judgments from authentic instruments and agreements, within the meaning of those regulations.[14]

The scope of this decision, particularly in light of the claim for uniform application of EU law, is unclear.

24) If one takes both the uniform application of EU law and the CJEU's findings in *TB* seriously, the decision reaches far beyond the issue of private divorces and would also affect parenthood cases and the application of the Parenthood Proposal: here, civil status officers also undertake a substantive examination of a case before making registrations or issuing public documents. They would thus fulfil the definition the CJEU has set out in *TB*. Civil status officers would consequently not only be bound by the jurisdiction rules (Art. 6 et seq. PP), but the documents issued by them would also have to be recognised as court decisions under Art. 24 et seq. PP. As the rules on the recognition of authentic documents in Art. 44 and 45 PP make clear, the European legislator did not intend for civil status authorities to be classified as courts and did not want their decisions to be recognised under Art. 24 et seq. PP (cf. above para. 21). In order to make this legislative objective clearer and to avoid the application of *TB*, the definition of 'court' in Art. 4(4) PP needs to be clarified.

25) On a policy level, the Group wants to draw attention to the fact that a possible application of *TB* in the context of parenthood and other areas of international family law would likely lead to future legislative cooperation between the Member States on these matters, in general, becoming even more

---

[13] CJEU 15 November 2022, Case C-646/20 (*Senatsverwaltung für Inneres und Sport, Standesamtsaufsicht v. TB*), ECLI:EU:C:2022:879, para. 48.

[14] CJEU 15 November 2022, Case C-646/20 (*Senatsverwaltung für Inneres und Sport, Standesamtsaufsicht v. TB*), ECLI:EU:C:2022:879, para. 59.

difficult. It would not be surprising if some Member States did not participate in a future Parenthood Regulation from the outset if a substantive examination of foreign documents (cf. Art. 41 PP) is also excluded in the case of documents issued by civil status officers because they are to be considered 'court' decisions – not to mention that these documents have no binding effect in their country of origin (see also below para. 145).

26) In order to counteract such a development and to provide clarity in matters on parenthood (regarding the applicability of the rules on jurisdiction in Chapter II and the rules on recognition in Chapters IV and V), the Group strongly urges the European legislator to clarify the definition of the term 'court'. This is the only way to prevent any authority that is competent in matters of parenthood under national law from falling under the broad definition of 'court', even if it only acts in extrajudicial and non-contentious proceedings, such as civil registrars.

Article 5
Competence in matters of parenthood within the Member States

This Regulation shall not affect the competence of the authorities of the Member States to deal with parenthood matters.

Comments

27) Art. 5 PP corresponds with Art. 2 of the Succession Regulation and Art. 2 of the Property Regulations for spouses and registered partners. The Group does not propose any amendments.

CHAPTER II
JURISDICTION

Article 6
General jurisdiction

In matters relating to parenthood, jurisdiction shall lie with the courts of the Member State:	
(a) of the habitual residence of the child at the time the court is seised, or	
	(aa) of the residence of the child if the habitual residence of the child at the time the court is seised cannot be determined, or
(b) of the nationality of the child at the time the court is seised, or	
(c) of the habitual residence of the respondent at the time the court is seised, or	(c) of the habitual residence *at the time the court is seised of the person or persons whose parenthood is affected by the proceedings*, or
	(cc) of the nationality at the time the court is seised of the person or persons whose parenthood is affected by the proceedings.
(d) of the habitual residence of either parent at the time the court is seised, or	~~(d) of the habitual residence of either parent at the time the court is seised, or~~
(e) of the nationality of either parent at the time the court is seised, or	~~(e) of the nationality of either parent at the time the court is seised, or~~
(f) of birth of the child.	~~(f) of birth of the child.~~

Comments

28) Art. 6 PP sets out the jurisdiction for court proceedings in matters relating to parenthood. It does not apply to court proceedings dealing with decisions of civil status officers setting up authentic instruments or registering the parenthood of the child, since those proceedings are no civil matters in the sense of Art. 3(1) PP (see below para. 169; see also above para. 21 regarding the need to clarify that civil status authorities issuing civil status documents do not constitute courts in the sense of Art. 4(4) PP and that Art. 6 et seq. PP therefore do not apply to them).

General goals of the jurisdictional rules

29) According to the Commission (cf. Recital 39), the jurisdictional rules are meant to promote the best interests of the child whose parenthood is at stake. This goal is to be accomplished by two principles: first, the grounds for jurisdiction are supposed to be based on a proximity to the child (cf. Recital 39). This goal is particularly evident in Art. 6(a) and (b) PP and is also pursued in the newly proposed Art. 6(aa) PP. Secondly, the child's access to justice should be facilitated by opening a variety of jurisdictional bases and providing various fallback options in Art. 7 to 9 PP in case a general jurisdiction cannot be established under Art. 6 PP. While these goals are convincing in principle, their implementation in Art. 6 to 9 PP can be improved.[15]

30) The potential multitude of available fora offered by Art. 6 PP can be particularly beneficial where the legal recognition of a parent-child relationship differs in the (available) fora. Even with the envisaged common conflict rules in Art. 16 et seq. PP, such cases can persist, for instance if a certain parent-child relationship is considered a public policy infringement in the sense of Art. 22 PP in one or more of the available fora (e.g. assisted reproduction; rare family forms, such as families with two female parents or transgender parents). In such cases the child or a parent can choose amongst the available fora and start proceedings in a more liberal forum.

31) Such advantages of wide jurisdictional rules have to be balanced with their disadvantages. Broad jurisdictional rules generally create the danger of forum shopping which could be used as a disruptive procedural strategy.[16]

---

[15] In subsequence, Recital 39 should be adapted.

[16] *Gössl*, 'Die Anerkennung der Elternschaft zwischen den Mitgliedstaaten der EU', *Forum Familienrecht* 2023, 101, 109; *González Beilfuss*, 'La proposition de Règlement européen en matière de filiation: analyse liminaire', *Revue trimestrielle de droit européen* 2023, 217.

Such rules can be particularly problematic if third parties can use them to bring frivolous lawsuits to disturb an existing (social) family unit (e.g. a person falsely claiming to be the biological father of a child). In matters relating to the termination of an existing parenthood, such situations might occur. On a general level, however, the threat of forum shopping is limited in parenthood matters as compared to other civil and family law matters, because parenthood matters tend to be litigated less frequently and confrontationally than other family matters. Furthermore, the incentives for forum shopping would be reduced considerably by the unification of the applicable law under Art. 16 et seq. PP.[17] Nevertheless, as detailed below, the Group is of the opinion that some of the proposed bases of jurisdiction seem to be exorbitant and should be deleted.

Deletion of indefinite jurisdiction at the child's place of birth, Art. 6(f) PP

32) First, Art. 6(f) PP, which opens jurisdiction at the child's place of birth indefinitely, appears to be exorbitant and should be deleted. The place of birth does not, in itself, possess a lasting proximity to the child. The exorbitant nature of this jurisdiction becomes particularly evident when considering that lit. (f) only has a specific relevance if the place of birth is neither the current habitual residence of the child nor corresponds to his or her nationality – otherwise jurisdiction could already be based on lit. (a) or (b).

33) The Group is mindful that a deletion of lit. (f) has a potentially unwanted policy implication, as the jurisdiction of the courts at the child's place of birth can be relevant in cases concerning assisted reproduction, in particular cases where methods of assisted reproduction are used that are not legally available in some Member States (e.g. surrogate motherhood, see above para. 30). In such cases, the place of birth can be where such a procedure has taken place and is legal. In this case, it is likely that the courts in that jurisdiction would recognise a legal parenthood based on such a procedure, while the home jurisdiction of the parents might deny such a parenthood as an infringement of public policy. If it is the desire of the legislator to enable a legal parent-child relationship in such cases, a deletion of lit. (f) would – at first glance – undermine this goal. However, as will be explained (below para. 34 et seq.), the inclusion of a new jurisdictional basis in lit. (aa) can adequately fulfil the desired policy goal.

---

[17] cf. *Válková*, 'The Commission Proposal for a Regulation on the Recognition of Parenthood and other Legislative Trends Affecting Legal Parenthood', *Rivista di diritto internazionale privato e processuale* 2023, 854, 889; *Fulchiron*, 'La proposition de règlement européen sur la filiation: coup de maître ou coup d'épée dans l'eau?', *Journal du droit international* 2023, 1171, 1177 et seq.

Jurisdiction at the child's (simple) residence, proposed Art. 6(aa) PP

34) If lit. (f) is deleted, according to the Group's proposal, a new lit. (aa) should be included to vest jurisdiction in the courts at the child's residence, however only if no habitual residence of the child can be established at the time the court is seised. This provision would address two main scenarios in which a habitual residence of the child cannot be determined at the time the court is seised.

35) The first of these instances is immediately after the child is born, but before the child is settled with the primary caregivers. In this situation, the Group's proposal would give parents the opportunity to seise the courts at the child's place of birth in order to establish parenthood shortly after birth. As the jurisdiction is based on the lack of a habitual residence 'at the time the court is seised', this jurisdiction would persist even if the families return to their home State during the proceedings and the child gains a habitual residence there. As mentioned (see above para. 33), this jurisdiction serves convincing policy considerations, e.g. in the context of assisted reproduction. The families can benefit from a forum at the place of birth whose public policy will probably align with more lenient assisted reproduction regulations in that Member State. However, unlike an indefinite jurisdiction at the child's place of birth under the current Art. 6(f) PP (see above para. 32), the suggested provision would be more narrowly tailored and would more specifically address those policy goals. The proposed Art. 6(aa) PP can therefore replace the current lit. (f). The second fact pattern for the proposed jurisdiction focuses on children who are refugees or internationally displaced persons and do not – for that reason – have a habitual residence. Since the proposed jurisdiction header would open jurisdiction at the residence of the child in these cases, the current Art. 7 PP should be deleted in consequence (see below para. 41, and para. 42 et seq. for changes to Art. 7 PP in case this proposal is not taken on).

Amendments to Art. 6(d) and (e) PP: no jurisdiction solely based on habitual residence or nationality of the parent not affected by the proceedings

36) Art. 6(d) and (e) PP open jurisdiction in the Member State of the habitual residence or nationality of either parent. In principle, provisions that offer jurisdiction based on circumstances relating to the potential parents instead of the child are important. This is because in some cases, proceedings that affect the parenthood of the child can take place before the birth of the child.[18] Additionally, a proximity of the forum to the potential parents affected by

[18] e.g. so-called pre-birth orders.

the proceedings can be of great benefit when it is necessary to raise evidence, foremost in the form of a blood sample. Acquiring such a sample across borders can be very difficult even under the European Regulation on the Taking of Evidence (Council Regulation (EC) 1206/2001 of 28 May 2001 on cooperation between the courts of the Member States in the taking of evidence in civil or commercial matters [2001] OJ L174/1), in particular if the person affected is not cooperative, because they do not want to become a legal parent. In such a case, courts with close proximity to the potential parent are best placed to acquire a blood sample and reach a timely decision.

37) These advantages, however, only justify a jurisdiction based on the habitual residence or nationality of the person or persons whose parenthood is affected by the proceedings. Art. 6(d) and (e) PP should be restricted accordingly. Currently they open jurisdiction also based on the habitual residence or nationality of a person whose parenthood is not affected by the proceedings. This becomes relevant if the parenthood of only one parent is addressed by the court (e.g. establishment or termination of fatherhood). Under the current wording of lit. (d) and (e), this person could bring proceedings in another Member State, simply because it is the Member State of the habitual residence or nationality of another parent whose parenthood is not addressed by the court (e.g. the mother). It is unclear what the residence or nationality of the mother has to do with proceedings to establish or terminate the fatherhood. The exorbitant nature of lit. (d) and (e) is particularly obvious when one takes into account that these provisions only come into play if the other parent (e.g. the mother), whose parenthood is not addressed in the court decision, does not share the child's habitual residence or nationality. Otherwise lit. (d) and (e) would open jurisdiction where lit. (a) or (b) already do so anyway. Lit. (d) and (e) should therefore be restricted to open jurisdiction at the habitual residence or in the home State of that person or those persons whose parenthood is affected by the proceedings. These rules are introduced in the amended lit. (c) (see also below para. 38) and the proposed lit. (cc) respectively. The inclusion of both habitual residence and nationality mirrors the parallelism of those connecting factors being used in lit. (a) and (b) in relation to the child.

Amendment to Art. 6(c) PP: indeterminacy of the term 'respondent'

38) The amendments proposed by the Group to the current lit. (c) and the introduction of a new lit. (cc) are also justified by the fact that the term 'respondent' in the current Art. 6(c) PP is unclear and should be deleted. The meaning of this term is unclear because parenthood proceedings do not necessarily operate in a (quasi-) contentious setting, and it might not be obvious to whom the term 'respondent' can refer. The term 'respondent'

seems to be based on a predetermined understanding of the applicable procedural law, which might not reflect the existing procedural laws of the Member States. Presumably, the 'respondent' is a person whose existing parenthood is challenged in the proceedings or whose parenthood is meant to be established in the proceedings against the will of the 'respondent'. Both types of proceedings would be covered by the proposed jurisdiction in the Member State of habitual residence or nationality of the person or persons whose parenthood is affected by the proceedings (amended lit. (c) and new lit. (cc)).

39) Abolishing the term 'respondent' in the jurisdictional context would also be helpful for cases where the person whose parenthood is addressed by the proceedings has died after conception (e.g. biological father dies before his fatherhood can be established; fatherhood of a legal father is challenged after his death;[19] post-mortal assisted reproduction). In these cases, the proposed wording would make clear that the habitual residence of the deceased person remains relevant as the basis of jurisdiction and not – for instance – the habitual residence of an heir of the deceased, who might be a party to the proceedings. In such a case, the phrase 'at the time the court is seised' should be read as 'at the time of death of the parent affected'. This matter could also be addressed in a Recital.

No inclusion of choice of court or entering an appearance

40) Because of the broad scope of jurisdiction already available in Art. 6 to 9 PP, no change appears necessary in relation to the current exclusion of jurisdiction by choice of court or by entering an appearance. For one thing, it is not clear who should choose the jurisdiction. Since the goal of parenthood proceedings is to establish who the legal parents of the child are, the choice could not be restricted to legal parents. Conversely, giving potential parents a choice could lead to abuse and would distract from the child-centred approach of the Parenthood Proposal. Additionally, the rules on jurisdiction in international family and succession law have so far only granted a limited choice of jurisdiction (e.g. Art. 5 et seq. of the Succession Regulation: nationality of deceased; Art. 10 of the Brussels IIb Regulation: Member States in which at least one of the holders of parental responsibility is habitually resident, in which the child had a former habitual residence or of which the child is a national). And they have complemented narrow rules of general jurisdiction (Art. 4 of the Succession Regulation: habitual residence of deceased at the time of death; Art. 7 of the Brussels IIb

[19] e.g. termination of fatherhood after the death of the legal father; cf. CJEU 13 October 2016, Case C-294/15 (*Edyta Mikołajczyk v. Marie Louise Czarnecka, Stefan Czarnecki*), ECLI:EU:C:2016:772.

Regulation: habitual residence of the child). In the Parenthood Proposal the general jurisdiction is already very wide. Therefore, there is neither a need to compensate a restrictive general jurisdiction with a choice of court nor is there a jurisdictional basis that is not yet available and that should be opened through a choice of court.

Article 7 **Jurisdiction based on the presence of the child**	~~**Article 7**~~ ~~**Jurisdiction based on the presence of the child**~~
Where jurisdiction cannot be determined on the basis of Article 6, the courts of the Member State where the child is present shall have jurisdiction.	~~Where jurisdiction cannot be determined on the basis of Article 6, the courts of the Member State where the child is present shall have jurisdiction.~~

Comments

Deletion of Art. 7 PP

41) Art. 7 to 9 PP set out jurisdictional bases that come into play when a jurisdiction cannot be established under Art. 6 PP. The Group suggests restricting these provisions. Art. 7 PP corresponds to Art. 11(1) of the Brussels IIb Regulation. It supplies a fallback jurisdiction based on the presence of the child for cases in which jurisdiction cannot be established in a Member State under Art. 6 PP. This can be particularly relevant for refugee children or internationally displaced children, i.e. in cases in which the child will likely not have a habitual residence. The proposed Art. 6(aa) PP would establish jurisdiction in these cases at the simple residence of the child and would, thus, fulfil the goals currently pursued by Art. 7 PP.[20] If the new Art. 6(aa) PP is introduced as suggested above, Art. 7 PP would become superfluous and should be deleted.[21]

Alternative wording in the event that deletion is refused

42) In case Art. 6(aa) PP is not introduced and Art. 7 PP is not deleted, the Group alternatively suggests rephrasing Art. 7 as follows:

---

[20] For the reasons, see Art. 6 PP, above para. 34 et seq.

[21] Recital 42 should be deleted in consequence.

Article 7
Jurisdiction based on the presence of the child

Where *the habitual residence of the child at the time the court is seised cannot be established and* jurisdiction cannot be determined on the basis of Article 6, the courts of the Member State where the child is present shall have jurisdiction.

Comments

43) To fulfil the above-mentioned goals, and in line with Art. 11(1) of the Brussels IIb Regulation,[22] Art. 7 PP should be restricted to cases in which the habitual residence of the child cannot be determined, e.g. because the child is a refugee or an internationally displaced person. Without such a restriction, Art. 7 PP could lead to an exorbitant jurisdiction. In its proposed form, Art. 7 PP would open a jurisdiction in cases that have no relevant connection to the EU (and therefore, there is no jurisdiction under Art. 6 PP in the EU). The current wording of Art. 7 PP opens jurisdiction, for example, for a family which is in a Member State for a holiday trip even though the family has a habitual residence outside of the EU and none of the family members have EU nationality. In such a case, Art. 7 PP seems exorbitant. There is no need for a jurisdiction within the EU. Instead, matters of parenthood can and should be addressed by a court in the third State where that family lives.

Article 8
Residual jurisdiction

Where no court of a Member State has jurisdiction pursuant to Articles 6 or 7, jurisdiction shall be determined, in each Member State, by the laws of that Member State.

~~**Article 8**~~
~~**Residual jurisdiction**~~

~~Where no court of a Member State has jurisdiction pursuant to Articles 6 or 7, jurisdiction shall be determined, in each Member State, by the laws of that Member State.~~

[22] cf. *Gottwald*, in 'Münchener Kommentar zum FamFG', 3rd edition, C.H. Beck, Munich, 2019, Art. 13 Brussels IIa Regulation para. 1 et seq.

Comments

Deletion of residual jurisdiction, Art. 8 PP

44) Art. 8 PP is equivalent to Art. 14 of the Brussels IIb Regulation.

45) In principle, it is commendable that the Parenthood Proposal intends to protect children from a lack of jurisdiction within the EU in order to facilitate the clarification of the children's parenthood. However, the rules in Art. 7 to 9 PP seem excessive in that they combine different approaches which are used for similar goals in the existing Regulations: the Brussels IIb Regulation uses a subsidiary jurisdiction based on the presence of the child and a residual jurisdiction based on Member State law (see Art. 11 and 14 of the Brussels IIb Regulation). Since passing the Maintenance Regulation, the residual jurisdiction based on national law has been abandoned in EU legislative texts. Instead, Art. 6 and 7 of the Maintenance Regulation provide an autonomous European subsidiary jurisdiction and a *forum necessitatis.* The Property Regulations for spouses and registered partners and the Succession Regulation only provide for a *forum necessitatis* (Art. 11 of all three Regulations). The combination of all three approaches in Art. 7 to 9 PP (residual jurisdiction under Member State law, autonomous European subsidiary jurisdiction and *forum necessitatis*) is unique to the Parenthood Proposal and seems excessive – particularly in view of the broad general jurisdiction under Art. 6 PP. Therefore, the Group suggests maintaining only the *forum necessitatis* in Art. 9 PP and the subsidiary jurisdiction suggested above for children whose habitual residence cannot be determined either in the proposed new Art. 6(aa) PP or – if the Group's proposal is not taken on – the amended Art. 7 PP. Those provisions can provide sufficient protection for children: Art. 6(aa) PP as a 'standardised' fallback if the child's habitual residence cannot be determined, and Art. 9 PP as the general, but restrictive, *forum necessitatis.* This would be in line with the approach taken in Art. 6 and 7 of the Maintenance Regulation. The residual jurisdiction in Art. 8 PP, conversely, should be deleted.[23] Its recourse to national law undermines the comprehensive nature of EU law.[24] The approach has been abandoned by the EU legislator since the Maintenance Regulation.

---

23 Recital 43 should be deleted in consequence.

24 cf. *Válková*, Rivista di diritto internazionale privato e processuale 2023, 854, 890.

Article 9
Forum necessitatis

Where no court of a Member State has jurisdiction pursuant to other provisions of this Regulation, the courts of a Member State may, on an exceptional basis, rule on parenthood matters if proceedings cannot reasonably be brought or conducted or would be impossible in a third State with which the case is closely connected.

The case must have a sufficient connection with the Member State of the court seised.

Comments

46) Art. 9 PP corresponds to Art. 7 of the Maintenance Regulation and Art. 11 of the Property Regulations for spouses and registered partners. It is equivalent to Art. 11 of the Succession Regulation.

Article 10
Incidental questions

1. If the outcome of proceedings in a matter not falling within the scope of this Regulation before a court of a Member State depends on the determination of an incidental question relating to parenthood, a court in that Member State may determine that question for the purposes of those proceedings even if that Member State does not have jurisdiction under this Regulation.

2. The determination of an incidental question pursuant to paragraph 1 shall produce effects only in the proceedings for which that determination was made.

Comments

47) The draft corresponds to Art. 16(1) and (2) of the Brussels IIb Regulation.

Article 11
Seising of a court

A court shall be deemed to be seised:

(a) at the time when the document instituting the proceedings or an equivalent document is lodged with the court, provided that the applicant has not subsequently failed to take the steps he or she was required to take to have service effected on the respondent;

(b) if the document has to be served before being lodged with the court, at the time when it is received by the authority responsible for service, provided that the applicant has not subsequently failed to take the steps he or she was required to take to have the document lodged with the court; or

(c) if the proceedings are instituted of the court's own motion, at the time when the decision to institute the proceedings is taken by the court, or, where such a decision is not required, at the time when the case is registered by the court.

Comments

48) The proposed provision corresponds to Art. 17 of the Brussels IIb Regulation, Art. 14 of the Property Regulations for spouses and registered partners and

Art. 14 of the Succession Regulation. Art. 11(a) and (b) PP correspond to Art. 32(1) of the Brussels Ia Regulation (Regulation (EU) 1215/2012 of 12 December 2012 on jurisdiction and the recognition and enforcement of judgments in civil and commercial matters [2012] OJ L351/1).

Article 12
Examination as to jurisdiction

Where a court of a Member State is seised of a case over which it has no jurisdiction as to the substance of the matter under this Regulation and over which a court of another Member State has jurisdiction as to the substance of the matter under this Regulation, it shall declare of its own motion that it has no jurisdiction.

Comments

49) The proposed provision is equivalent to Art. 18 of the Brussels IIb Regulation. It is similar to Art. 15 of the Property Regulations for spouses and registered partners and Art. 15 of the Succession Regulation. The latter do not include the restriction 'and over which a court of another Member State has jurisdiction as to the substance of the matter under this Regulation'.

Article 13
Examination as to admissibility

1. Where a respondent habitually resident in a State other than the Member State where the proceedings were instituted does not enter an appearance, the court with jurisdiction shall stay the proceedings so long as it is not shown that the respondent has been able to receive the document instituting the proceedings or an equivalent document in sufficient time to enable the respondent to arrange for a defence, or that all necessary steps have been taken to this end.

2. Article 22 of Regulation (EU) 2020/1784 shall apply instead of paragraph 1 of this Article if the document instituting the proceedings or an equivalent document had to be transmitted from one Member State to another pursuant to that Regulation.

3. Where Regulation (EU) 2020/1784 is not applicable, Article 15 of the Hague Convention of 15 November 1965 on the service abroad of judicial and extrajudicial documents in civil or commercial matters shall apply if the document instituting the proceedings or an equivalent document had to be transmitted abroad pursuant to that Convention.

Comments

50) Art. 13(1) PP corresponds to Art. 19(1) of the Brussels IIb Regulation, Art. 16(1) of the Property Regulations for spouses and registered partners, Art. 16(1) of the Succession Regulation and Art. 28(2) of the Brussels Ia Regulation.

51) Art. 13(2) and (3) PP correspond with Art. 19(2) and (3) of the Brussels IIb Regulation, Art. 16(2) and (3) of the Property Regulations for spouses and registered partners, Art. 16(2) and (3) of the Succession Regulation and Art. 28(3) and (4) of the Brussels Ia Regulation, except for the references in the Brussels IIb Regulation, the Property Regulations for spouses and registered partners, the Succession Regulation and the Brussels Ia Regulation to the 2007 Service of Documents Regulation (Council Regulation (EC) 1393/2007 of 13 November 2007 on the service in the Member States of judicial and extrajudicial documents in civil or commercial matters [2007] OJ L324/79), having been adapted to the 2020 recast of the Service of Documents Regulation (Regulation (EU) 2020/1784 of 25 November 2020 on the service in the Member States of judicial and extrajudicial documents in civil or commercial matters [2020] OJ L405/40).

Article 14 **Lis pendens**	
1. Where proceedings involving the same cause of action and between the same parties are brought before courts of different Member States, any court other than the court first seised shall of its own motion stay its proceedings until such time as the jurisdiction of the court first seised is established.	1. Where proceedings involving the ~~same cause of action and between the same parties~~ *parenthood of the same child* are brought before courts of different Member States, any court other than the court first seised shall of its own motion stay its proceedings until such time as the jurisdiction of the court first seised is established.
2. In the cases referred to in paragraph 1, upon request by a court seised of the dispute, any other court seised shall without delay inform the requesting court of the date when it was seised.	
3. Where the jurisdiction of the court first seised is established, any court other than the court first seised shall decline jurisdiction in favour of the court first seised.	3. Where the jurisdiction of the court first seised is established, any court other than the court first seised shall decline jurisdiction in favour of the court first seised *if it is seised of the same cause of action. Any court other than the court first seised shall stay its proceedings if it is seised of a cause of action for which the cause of action dealt with by the court first seised is only a preliminary question.*

Comments

52) Art. 14 PP addresses the coordination of proceedings and opposing *lis pendens*. It is equivalent to Art. 17 of the Property Regulations for spouses and registered partners. Art. 14 PP corresponds to Art. 29 of the Brussels Ia Regulation. Art. 14(1) and (3) PP correspond to Art. 20(1) and (3) of the Brussels IIb Regulation and Art. 17 of the Succession Regulation. Art. 14 PP, however, is not sufficiently adapted to the specificities of parenthood proceedings.

Extension of lis pendens: deletion of the phrase 'same cause of action and between the same parties' in Art. 14(1) PP

53) Since the Parenthood Proposal only affects the establishment and termination of parenthood, the restriction to proceedings relating to the 'same cause of action' should be deleted. It is superfluous. Additionally, it could raise misguided questions, such as whether the establishment and termination of the parenthood of the same person are 'the same cause of action' or whether the termination of the parenthood of one person is 'the same cause of action' as the establishment of the parenthood of another person. As parenthood over a child is an overarching question where there is an interplay of the different potential parents, proceedings relating to the parenthood of one (potential) parent can generally affect the parenthood of all other (potential) parents.

54) For similar reasons, the phrase 'between the same parties' should be deleted. Parenthood proceedings generally establish or terminate parenthood with *erga omnes* effects, i.e. they affect not only the parties to the proceedings but also third parties. Therefore, the *lis pendens* rule should not be limited to the parties to the proceedings. Instead, it should extend to any proceedings 'involving the parenthood of the same child', irrespective of the identity of the parties to the proceedings. As the parenthood of one (potential) parent can generally affect the parenthood of all other (potential) parents, only one court at a time should address the parenthood over a child. Irreconcilable decisions can be reached even in proceedings relating to potentially different causes of action and between different parties. This proposed change is in line with Art. 20(2) of the Brussels IIb Regulation, which also relates to a legal issue (parental responsibility) with potential third-party effects.

Distinction as to the consequences of lis pendens in Art. 14(3) PP

55) If Art. 14(1) PP is extended in the proposed way, Art. 14(3) PP also has to be adapted. Since the Group suggests extending *lis pendens* beyond proceedings relating to the same cause of action and between the same parties, the reaction of a court later seised has to be differentiated. If the proceedings before the court later seised involve the same cause of action, a decision of the court later seised is superfluous at best, and potentially irreconcilable with the decision of the court first seised. The court later seised shall therefore decline jurisdiction. If the proceedings before the court second seised relate to a cause of action for which the issues addressed by the court first seised only constitute a preliminary question, the decision by the court later seised is not superfluous but should not contradict the decision of the court first seised. In these circumstances, the court later seised should stay the proceedings until either the court first seised has rendered a decision or until it has been established that the proceedings before

the court later seised are not related to the first proceedings in a way that they would create the danger of irreconcilable judgments.

Article 15 **Right of children to express their views**	~~**Article 15**~~ ~~**Right of children to express their views**~~
1. When exercising their jurisdiction under this Regulation, the courts of the Member States shall, in accordance with national law and procedure, provide children below the age of 18 years whose parenthood is to be established and who are capable of forming their own views, with a genuine and effective opportunity to express their views, either directly or through a representative or an appropriate body.	~~1.When exercising their jurisdiction under this Regulation, the courts of the Member States shall, in accordance with national law and procedure, provide children below the age of 18 years whose parenthood is to be established and who are capable of forming their own views, with a genuine and effective opportunity to express their views, either directly or through a representative or an appropriate body.~~
2. Where the court, in accordance with national law and procedure, gives children below the age of 18 years an opportunity to express their views in accordance with this Article, the court shall give due weight to the views of the children in accordance with their age and maturity.	~~2.Where the court, in accordance with national law and procedure, gives children below the age of 18 years an opportunity to express their views in accordance with this Article, the court shall give due weight to the views of the children in accordance with their age and maturity.~~

Comments

Deletion or alternatively modification of Art. 15 PP

56) Art. 15 PP establishes a right for the child to be heard in parenthood proceedings. The provision is inspired by Art. 21 of the Brussels IIb Regulation. However, since the usefulness of such a provision in parenthood matters is unclear, the Group primarily proposes to delete Art. 15 PP entirely.[25] See the reasoning below in para. 58 et seq.

---

[25] Recital 49 should be deleted in consequence.

57) If the provision is not deleted it should at least be redrafted as follows:

Article 15
Right of children to express their views

1. When exercising their jurisdiction under this Regulation *in proceedings on the termination of parenthood and on adoption*, the courts of the Member States shall, in accordance with national law and procedure, provide children ~~below the age of 18 years whose parenthood is to be established and~~ who are capable of forming their own views, with a genuine and effective opportunity to express their views, either directly or through a representative or an appropriate body.

2. Where the court, in accordance with national law and procedure, gives children ~~below the age of 18 years~~ an opportunity to express their views in accordance with this Article, the court shall give due weight to the views of the children in accordance with their age and maturity.

3. Paragraph 1 shall not affect the right of children to be heard in other proceedings under the law of the Member State of the court seised.

58) The scope of the duty to hear children should be restricted. Art. 15 PP corresponds to Art. 21 of the Brussels IIb Regulation. However, the context in both Regulations is different. Art. 21 of the Brussels IIb Regulation addresses the right of the child to express their views in proceedings on parental responsibility. In such proceedings, the best interests of the child are of paramount importance. The best interest of the child is a core factual consideration in a court's decision on parental responsibility. To assess these interests, hearing the views of the child

is crucial. The factual question of which parental responsibility arrangement is best for the child should not be decided without hearing the child.

No general need to hear the child in proceedings on the establishment of parenthood

59) In parenthood proceedings the situation is different. Regarding the establishment of parenthood, the best interests of the child are generally irrelevant to the substantive law of parenthood. In proceedings on the establishment of parenthood, generally, the only factual questions relevant to the substantive law relate to the genetic descent of the child or to the consent of the potential parents or gamete donors.[26] Hearing a child is of no benefit to determine these questions and, in consequence, to the decision of the court.

60) Conversely, hearing the child could even be of detriment to the child in proceedings on the establishment of parenthood: if the best interests of the child are irrelevant to the allocation of legal parenthood, it could create false expectations and disappointment if the child is heard, but that hearing subsequently has no relevance for the decision of the court. What is more, hearing a child on who their parent should be can create psychological strain and conflicts of loyalties for the child. Additionally, hearing the child can delay the proceedings, particularly in international proceedings, and can be used as a dilatory tactic if the relationship between the potential parents is strained.

Hearing the child in proceedings on termination of parenthood and adoption

61) Unlike in proceedings on the establishment of parenthood, hearing a child can, however, be crucial in adoption proceedings and proceedings on the termination of parenthood. This is because in these proceedings, the best interests of the child or similar factual questions[27] can be relevant to the substantive decision of the court. In assessing these questions, the perspective of the child can be of added value and should not be ignored. This can be seen as an argument for retaining Art. 15 PP in relation to those proceedings. However, the Group believes that it can be trusted that national legislators and individual

---

[26] e.g. the waiver of parenthood by a gamete donor; the consent to an artificial reproduction given by the partner of the birth parent.

[27] e.g. Section 1600(2) of the German Civil Code: a contestation of the fatherhood brought by the biological father requires that there must not be a 'social and family relationship' between the child and the legal father.

courts will ensure a hearing of the child in these situations on their own accord even without an explicit provision in the Parenthood Proposal. The EU should respect the procedural autonomy of the Member States and focus on issues of private international law. Where a court fails to hear the child, the recognition of the subsequent decision can be refused under the public policy exception (see below para. 124 et seq.). Therefore, the Group maintains the deletion of Art. 15 PP as its primary proposal. If Art. 15 PP should remain in the Parenthood Proposal, the duty to hear the child should at least be restricted to proceedings on the termination of parenthood and to adoption proceedings. In addition, a third paragraph should be included to clarify that a hearing of the child is not prohibited in other cases. The proposed wording is inspired by Art. 12(2) of the Succession Regulation.

62) If Art. 15 PP is not deleted, the reference to children 'below the age of 18 years' should be removed in Art. 15(1) and (2) PP. Presumably, this phrase is meant to highlight that children should be heard even if they are underage. However, the text could also be understood to restrict the right to be heard to minors, while excluding – *e contrario* – the hearing of children above that age, even though parenthood matters can arise irrespective of the age of the child.

CHAPTER III
APPLICABLE LAW

Article 16
Universal application

Any law designated as applicable by this Regulation shall be applied whether or not it is the law of a Member State.

Comments

63) The provision is part of the European acquis. It corresponds, for example, to Art. 4 of the Rome III Regulation (Council Regulation (EU) 1259/2010 of 20 December 2010 implementing enhanced cooperation in the area of the law applicable to divorce and legal separation [2010] OJ L343/10), Art. 20 of the Succession Regulation and Art. 20 of the Property Regulations for spouses and registered partners.

Article 17 **Applicable law**	**~~Applicable law~~*Establishment of parenthood***
1. The law applicable to the establishment of parenthood shall be the law of the State of the habitual residence of the person giving birth at the time of birth or, where the habitual residence of the person giving birth at the time of birth cannot be determined, the law of the State of birth of the child.	1. The law applicable to the establishment of parenthood *at the time of birth* shall be the law of the State of the habitual residence of the person giving birth at the time of birth or, where the habitual residence of the person giving birth at the time of birth cannot be determined, the law of the State of birth of the child.
2. Notwithstanding paragraph 1, where the applicable law pursuant to paragraph 1 results in the establishment of parenthood as regards only one parent, the law of the State of nationality of that parent or of the second parent, or the law of the State of birth of the child, may apply to the establishment of parenthood as regards the second parent.	2. ~~Notwithstanding paragraph 1, where the applicable law pursuant to paragraph 1 results in the establishment of parenthood as regards only one parent, the law of the State of nationality of that parent or of the second parent, or the law of the State of birth of the child, may apply to the establishment of parenthood as regards the second parent.~~

The law applicable to the establishment of parenthood after the time of birth shall be the law of the State of the habitual residence of the child at the time when parenthood is established or, where the habitual residence of the child cannot be determined, in relation to each parent the law of the State of this parent's habitual residence at the time when parenthood is established. Where the habitual residence of a parent cannot be determined, the law of the State of his or her nationality shall apply.

3. As far as the law applicable according to paragraph 1 or paragraph 2 restricts the possibility to establish parenthood based on the parents' sex or excludes the establishment of parenthood for children born out of wedlock, parenthood can be established according to

(a) the law of the habitual residence of the parent affected by the restriction, or

(b) the law of the State of nationality of the parent affected by the restriction, or

(c) the law of the State of birth of the child.

Comments

64) Art. 17 PP contains the general rule for determining the law governing parenthood. The Group suggests several amendments.

Differentiation: establishment of parenthood at the time of birth and after the time of birth, amendments to Art. 17(1) PP and a new Art. 17(2) PP

65) Art. 17(1) PP refers to the habitual residence of the person giving birth at the time of birth. This approach is a good starting point for determining the applicable law. It is a clear-cut rule that is easy to apply in practice by public registrars (and judges) since the vast majority of children are born in the country where the birth mother has her habitual residence. On top of this, it solves the problematic cases which arise in this context (e.g. birth of a child while the mother stays abroad for a limited period of time, or birth of a child by a surrogate mother while the intended parents from another country want to bring home their child immediately after birth). One could wonder whether choosing the child's habitual residence as the main connecting factor would be preferable. However, the weakness of a rule based on the habitual residence of a child is that it is sometimes hard to determine at the time of birth, and in the first weeks or months thereafter, whether the child has already established a habitual residence.[28]

66) Nevertheless, the approach chosen by the Parenthood Proposal does not lead to appropriate solutions in all scenarios. The first significant problem is that, according to Art. 17(1) PP, the connecting factor for the applicable law (habitual residence of the person giving birth) is unchangeable because it is fixed forever at the time of birth. However, there will be a whole series of cases where this solution is not appropriate because it does not lead to the application of a national legal system that has a material connection with the case at hand and is in line with the (legitimate) expectations of the parties.

> **Example**: An unmarried German woman has her habitual residence in France, where her child is born. Three years later, she permanently moves to Germany, where a German man recognises the child. According to the current Art. 17(1) PP, French law would apply to this acknowledgment of parenthood, although this case no longer has a real connection to France. Under French law, the consent of the mother is not necessary for the valid recognition of parenthood, but under the circumstances of this case, the German mother can rightly expect that the applicable law will now be German law, according to which recognition of parenthood is only valid if the mother gives her consent. Furthermore, according to the Parenthood Proposal, French law would apply to the contestation of parenthood, although the parents and child are German citizens living in Germany.

[28] On the possibility that a child might not have a habitual residence, cf. CJEU 2 April 2009, Case C-523/07 (*A*), ECLI:EU:C:2009:225, para. 43.

67) Apart from this, it is not very clear what is meant by the phrase in Art. 17(2) PP 'where the applicable law pursuant to paragraph 1 results in the establishment of parenthood as regards only one parent'. On the one hand, one could read this passage as referring to cases in which a child, under a certain national law, permanently has no possibility to be assigned to more than one legal parent (e.g. laws which forbid the establishment of parenthood to the father if a child was born out of wedlock). On the other hand, this expression could be understood in the broader sense that the recourse to Art. 17(2) PP is permissible as long as the law applicable according to Art. 17(1) PP provides the child with only one legal parent (although, in principle, it would be possible to assign the child a second legal parent if the corresponding material conditions of that law were fulfilled).

68) Foremost, Art. 17(2) PP seems to address a situation in which the applicable law does not allow co-motherhood (cf. Recital 52). But even in such cases where a child is born to a same-sex couple and the applicable law only accepts the parenthood of the birth mother (but not that of a co-mother), a second parenthood could still be established by way of an acknowledgment of fatherhood. Therefore, in most instances, only specific persons cannot legally be established as the second parent – mostly because of their gender – while the parenthood of some other person is usually – hypothetically – possible. Having this in mind, the phrase 'where the applicable law pursuant to paragraph 1 results in the establishment of parenthood as regards only one parent' cannot merely refer to the (relatively rare) cases where a national law *permanently* bars a child from having two legal parents. The Parenthood Proposal rather has to be understood to the effect that *as long as* the law applicable under Art. 17(1) PP leads to the establishment of one parent only a recourse to Art. 17(2) PP is possible.

69) Furthermore, there is some doubt as to what the phrase in Art. 17(2) PP means that a law 'may apply to the establishment of parenthood'. Presumably, by choosing this expression, the Commission wants to make clear that the application of Art. 17(2) PP is not automatic and obligatory, but discretionary. However, it is unclear who should have the authority to exercise this discretion: each judge or each public registrar or only the Member States? Moreover, such an understanding of Art. 17(2) PP would lead to the parenthood of a child being assessed differently depending on the Member State and the court or authority which has to decide on the issue of parenthood. This would be diametrically opposed to the aim of the Parenthood Proposal, which is to harmonise the assessment of a child's parenthood throughout Europe. Different individual assessments by the courts of different Member States must be limited to the recognised exceptional instruments, such as the public policy exception. It would be advisable to clarify this point in a Recital or otherwise. Such a clarification would also be advisable for the new Art. 17(3) PP, which, according to the Group's suggestion, should replace the existing Art. 17(2) PP.

70) As a result, in a number of cases, the law applicable to the establishment of the second parent is determined pursuant to Art. 17(2) PP, which offers a variety of alternative connecting factors which, in turn, can lead to different legal systems (and therefore to different material results). The alternative applicability of different legal systems to a parenthood of one child is, for example, already known to German private international law and has led to many intricate problems which should be avoided.

> **Example:** A German woman living in Germany gives birth to a child in May 2023. Her marriage to a Polish national has been legally ended by divorce in April 2023. A German man, the mother's new partner, declares the acknowledgment of paternity one month after the child's birth with the mother's consent.

71) According to Art. 17(1) PP, German law is applicable because of the habitual residence of the mother of the child. Under German law, the mother's husband automatically is the child's father (Section 1592(1) of the German Civil Code) only if the man is still married to the child's mother at the time of birth. In the example mentioned above, this is not the case due to the prior divorce, so according to German law, the child initially has the mother as his or her only parent at the time of birth. Therefore, the new German partner is free to acknowledge paternity according to German law as applicable under Art. 17(1) PP.

72) At the same time, however, Art. 17(2) PP would be applicable and can lead to the application of other legal regimes: at the time of birth, Art. 17(1) PP 'results in the establishment of parenthood as regards only one parent' (here: the mother). Therefore, under Art. 17(2) PP, the law of the State of the nationality of the 'second parent' would be applicable as well. The Polish ex-husband of the birth mother would be regarded as the child's father: under Polish law of parenthood, the (former) husband of the birth mother is automatically the child's legal father if the child is born within 300 days of the dissolution of the marriage. Thus, under Polish law, it is not the new German partner willing to recognise the child who will be the legal father but rather the mother's (Polish) ex-husband. In such cases, it is therefore unclear which rule is to be given preference: Art. 17(1) PP or Art. 17(2) PP. If one applies a priority principle and gives preference to the (automatic) fatherhood of the Polish ex-husband, which takes effect immediately at the birth of the child, this result will be very inconvenient since, in most cases, the new partner and not the ex-husband will be the genetic and social father of the child. Nevertheless, he would be forced to contest the paternity of the ex-husband before being able to acknowledge the paternity of the child.

73) To avoid the conflicts and uncertainties exemplified above, Art. 17(1) PP should be restricted to the establishment of parenthood 'at the time of birth'.

Most legal systems try to determine (whenever possible) parenthood from the very beginning at the exact time of the birth of a child, and therefore, many substantive rules come into play at this moment. That is true for the (more or less universally accepted) *mater semper certa est* rule (mother is the person who gives birth to a child) and the *pater est* rule (father of a child is the husband of the birth mother at the time of birth). Since the child has a fundamentally strong bond with the birth mother, applying the law of the State of her habitual residence is justified. However, immediately after birth, the child might be separated from the birth mother, and therefore the child's habitual residence should be decisive from then on. Furthermore, it would not be appropriate to further apply the law of the State of the habitual residence of the birth mother for an indeterminate period of time after birth. If the child is acknowledged three years after it was born, it would not meet the legitimate expectations of the parties and would not lead to the application of a legal system that has a material connection with the case at hand if the law determined by Art. 17(1) PP were still applicable, although the child might have moved to another country (cf. example mentioned in para. 66 above) or might have been separated from the birth mother (for example, in cases of surrogacy). Therefore, after the initial allocation of parenthood at birth, the applicable law should no longer be determined by the mother's habitual residence at the time of birth but by the child's habitual residence – as proposed by the new Art. 17(2) PP. This approach is in line with the philosophy of other European Regulations on family law, according to which the main connecting factor in modern international family law should be the habitual residence of the person(s) concerned – which, in this case, is mainly the child.

74) The phrase in the new Art. 17(1) PP 'law applicable to the establishment of parenthood at the time of birth of the child' is therefore meant to be taken literally: it encompasses the establishment of parenthood by operation of law and by prenatal declarations (e.g. prenatal recognition of parenthood). If a person, however, wants to acknowledge the child any time after the birth of the child, Art. 17(1) PP should no longer be applicable. Instead, the applicable law would be determined by the proposed Art. 17(2) PP.

75) In circumstances where the child's habitual residence cannot be determined for the purpose of the new Art. 17(2) PP (which can especially be the case right after birth), the Group suggests resorting to the habitual residence of the putative parent affected as a subsidiary connecting factor. However, where the parent's habitual residence can also not be determined, the law of the State of his or her nationality should apply. Multinationality is currently addressed insufficiently in Recital 41, which needs thorough revision. In an additional Recital, it should be made clear that applying the law of the State of a parent's nationality is only a last resort in extraordinary circumstances where the habitual residence neither of the child nor of the parent can be determined.

Avoiding the application of discriminatory national laws: rewriting Art. 17(2) PP

76) The Group welcomes, in principle, that the existing Art. 17(2) PP offers a set of alternative connecting factors in order to avoid the application of a discriminatory national law. However, the scope of this rule is too wide, and its application should not be left to the discretion of each Member State or even each judge or public registrar. The underlying favouring tendency, however, should be maintained, but the provision should be tailored more precisely to cases where it is really necessary and appropriate to provide alternative connecting factors, which should be applicable automatically and *ex officio*, in order to avoid the application of a discriminatory national law.

77) The new Art. 17(3) PP is in line with Art. 21 of the EU Charter of Fundamental Rights which prohibits any discrimination based on sex or birth. Its purpose is, in principle, the same as that of the existing Art. 17(2) PP, but it addresses the instances more clearly in which it should be applied. The new Art. 17(3) PP would, in particular, be applicable if the law determined by the new Art. 17(1) PP or Art. 17(2) PP does not allow co-motherhood or when, for (certain groups of) children born out of wedlock, the establishment of fatherhood is excluded (e.g. by national laws which restrict the establishment of fatherhood for children born out of wedlock, conceived in adultery, or for children conceived by incest). However, the suggested rule does not enforce a parenthood where a national law intentionally and for non-discriminatory purposes leaves open a parenthood position. This – for instance – would be the case in the example mentioned above in para. 70, where German law purposefully does not assign paternity to the ex-husband but leaves open that parenthood position in order for a new partner to be able to acknowledge paternity directly. The new rule, therefore, will avoid, to a large extent, the problems that can arise if several legal systems are applicable simultaneously.

78) It is to be noted that the wording of the first alternative of Art. 17(2) PP ('*restricts* the possibility to establish parenthood based on the parents' sex') is slightly different from the wording of the second alternative ('*excludes* the establishment of parenthood for children born out of wedlock'). The philosophy behind this distinction is that, in the case of same-sex (married or unmarried) parents, there is no justification for assigning the child to its parents according to different, i.e. more 'restrictive', rules than in the case of different-sex (married or unmarried) parents. In contrast, the birth of children within or outside of marriage constitutes a legitimate criterion for certain distinctions: most legal systems automatically assign a child to the birth mother's partner only if he or she is married to the birth mother, but not if there is only a de facto relationship between the parents. This is not

intended to discriminate against unmarried parents compared to married parents; instead, a de facto relationship is not considered a sufficiently certain criterion on which an automatic allocation of the child to one parent can be based.

79) Therefore, certain restrictions in the establishment of parenthood that address the lack of a formalised criterion on which to base parenthood (i.e. marriage) do not appear discriminatory and do not warrant a deviation from the normal application of Art. 17(1) and (2) PP. However, there is clear discrimination against children born out of wedlock if a legal system does not provide any possibility at all for such children in general or for certain groups of children born out of wedlock to be assigned to a second legal parent (i.e. the father). These are the cases envisaged by the phrase 'excludes', which should be addressed by the special conflicts rule proposed in Art. 17(3) PP. Admittedly, this relatively high threshold leaves out cases where, for children born out of wedlock, the establishment of parenthood is only restricted in a discriminatory way, i.e. beyond what is necessary to address the lack of a formalised partnership, but is not entirely excluded in the sense of Art. 17(3) PP. Such cases are, however, difficult to capture in a general formula. They should therefore be left to the general public policy rule (Art. 22 PP).

80) In contrast to the original Art. 17(2) PP, the new Art. 17(3) PP does not allow to resort to the 'law of the State of nationality of that parent'. Instead – apart from the law of the State of nationality of the second parent – it allows to resort to the law of the State of the second parent's habitual residence and to the law of the State of birth of the child.

81) Applying the 'law of the State of nationality of that parent', as the current Art. 17(2) PP suggests, would be very unusual and – at closer inspection – inappropriate.

> **Example**: A Spanish woman married to a German woman (both living in Germany) gives birth to a child. Applicable is, according to Art. 17(1) PP, German law since 'the person giving birth' has her habitual residence in Germany. According to German law, the Spanish woman is the legal mother according to Section 1591 of the German Civil Code since she gave birth to the child. But German law does not allow for co-motherhood outside of adoption. Therefore, according to the initial proposal of Art. 17(2) PP, Spanish law could be applied to the German wife since Spain is the State of nationality of 'that parent' ('that parent' being the Spanish birth mother). But why should Spanish law be applied to the parenthood of a German person living in Germany? The fact that she is married to a Spanish national is not a sufficient

connection to justify this result. It is a far-fetched solution that does not take into account the fundamental question of which legal system has a real link to the question at hand.

82) Instead, it is more in line with the philosophy of the Parenthood Proposal and the existing European Regulations in the area of family law to allow – apart from the law of the State of nationality of the second parent in question – to resort to the law of this person's habitual residence. Additionally, Art. 17(3) PP – in line with the original wording of Art. 17(2) PP – also allows the application of the law of the State where the child is born. The Group suggests conceiving the connecting factors in Art. 17(3)(a) to (c) PP as non-hierarchical alternatives. The alternative application is intended to make it easier for civil status registrars and judges to determine the applicable law and, if possible, to apply their own law.

Article 17a
Termination of parenthood

The law applicable to the termination of parenthood shall be

(a) the law under which parenthood was established according to Article 17, or

(b) the law of the State of the habitual residence of the child at the time of termination of parenthood.

Comments

83) The Parenthood Proposal does not address the termination of parenthood specifically. The Group suggests introducing a special conflict rule for this issue.

Introduction of a specific rule on termination of parenthood: a new Art. 17a PP

84) Art. 4(3) and 18(a) PP show that the term 'establishment of parenthood' in the Parenthood Proposal also covers the 'contestation of parenthood'.

Therefore, the law applicable to the contestation of parenthood is also meant to be determined by Art. 17 PP. To clarify the position of the Regulation, the question of which law is applicable to the contestation of parenthood should be addressed directly in a specific article. The contestation of parenthood does not automatically follow the same logic as the previous establishment of parenthood.

85) The underlying idea of the new Art. 17a(a) PP is that the same national law which was applicable for the establishment of legal parenthood (for example, at the time of birth by way of the *pater est* rule or at the time of an acknowledgment at a later stage in life) should also govern the contestation of parenthood. This is, in principle, only a clarification and is in line with the existing solution of the Parenthood Proposal.

86) Apart from resorting to the law under which parenthood was established, it should also be possible to contest parenthood in accordance with the law of the State of the child's habitual residence at the time of termination. First of all, the underlying principle of the Proposal's chapter on the applicable law should be that parenthood is governed, in general, by the law of the State of the child's habitual residence, cf. the new Art. 17(2) PP. Furthermore, the application of the law of the child's habitual residence usually allows courts to apply their own law (principle of harmonisation of forum and *ius*) since judicial proceedings concerning contestation of parenthood are usually instituted in the country where the child has his or her habitual residence (otherwise getting the necessary blood samples or witnesses can be very difficult). The principle laid down in lit. (b) also ensures that all persons (permanently) living in one country are treated the same way.

87) The new Art. 17a PP does not use the word 'contestation' but the somewhat broader term 'termination' of parenthood. This follows from the fact that contestation of parenthood is traditionally associated with contestation procedures before a court. However, in some legal systems, other instruments for terminating an existing parenthood also play an important role. For example, some national laws allow an acknowledgment of paternity for a child who already has a legal father without first challenging the existing legal paternity in court proceedings. Such an acknowledgment (in German: '*vaterschaftsdurchbrechende Anerkennung*') has two sides: first, there must be a valid acknowledgment of paternity (this question is covered by Art. 17 PP), and second, this acknowledgment terminates an existing legal fatherhood (this question should be covered by the new Art. 17a PP). The alternative would be to stick to the term 'contestation' and clarify in a Recital that this expression is to be understood broadly.

Article 18
Scope of the applicable law

The law designated by this Regulation as the law applicable to the establishment of parenthood shall govern, in particular:	The law designated by this Regulation as the law applicable to the establishment *or termination* of parenthood shall govern, in particular:
(a) the procedures to establish or contest parenthood;	(a) the ~~procedures~~ *requirements which have to be met in order* to establish or ~~contest~~ *terminate* parenthood;
(b) the binding legal effect and/or the evidentiary effects of authentic instruments;	~~(b) the binding legal effect and/or the evidentiary effects of authentic instruments;~~
(c) the standing of persons in proceedings involving the establishment or contestation of parenthood;	(c) ~~the standing of persons in proceedings involving the establishment or contestation of parenthood;~~ *the right to establish or terminate parenthood;*
(d) any time limits to establish or contest parenthood.	(d) any time limits to establish or ~~contest~~ *terminate* parenthood;
	(e) rules which raise presumptions of law or determine the burden of proof;
	(f) the question of whether an act establishing or terminating parenthood must be received by a certain person or authority.

Comments

88) With Art. 18 PP, the Proposal clarifies the scope of the applicable law determined by Art. 17 PP (and Art. 17a PP, if a special conflict rule for the termination of parenthood, as proposed by the Group, is adopted by the European legislator). The list provided in Art. 18 PP is not exhaustive ('in particular') but rather contains only some of the issues which are covered by

the law applicable to the establishment (Art. 17 PP) or termination (Art. 17a PP) of parenthood.

89) In general, the Group welcomes the approach of the Commission, which was also applied in other European instruments containing conflict rules, for example, in Art. 12 of the Rome I Regulation (Regulation (EC) 593/2008 of 17 June 2008 on the law applicable to contractual obligations [2008] OJ L177/6), Art. 23 of the Succession Regulation and Art. 27 of the Property Regulations for spouses and registered partners. Such a positive list of issues covered by the applicable law helps European citizens and the Member State courts and authorities to characterise issues which could potentially fall within the scope of other conflict rules.

90) However, some of the issues mentioned in the list of Art. 18 PP raise concerns, in particular, the delineation between the applicable substantive law, which can be a foreign law according to Art. 17 and 17a PP (*lex causae*), and the procedural law, which will always be the law of the respective forum (*lex fori*).

Retaining the lex fori principle: clarifying Art. 18(a) PP

91) According to the current wording of Art. 18(a) PP, the 'procedures to establish or contest parenthood' should be part of the law applicable to parenthood under Art. 17 PP.

92) This characterisation is potentially misleading. It is a well-established principle of private international law in and outside the European Union that each court or authority applies its own procedural law, even if the pertinent conflict rules provide for the application of foreign substantive law: *forum regit processum*. So far, the European legislator has not questioned the *lex fori* principle. All other European Regulations in the area of private international law determine only the applicable substantive law and leave the applicable procedural law to the *lex fori*. This traditional approach is sensible[29] because the court organisation is often aligned with the procedural rules of the forum. Furthermore, procedure is strongly linked with public law – hence, one could even doubt whether the European legislator has competence under Art. 81 of the Treaty on the Functioning of the European Union to harmonise the law applicable to procedure and, in particular, to force Member State courts and authorities to apply foreign procedural law.

93) Against this background, the Group understands the Commission's Proposal to the effect that only the substantive requirements for establishing or terminating parenthood are governed by the applicable law. Therefore, this point

[29] See, in general, the justification of the *lex fori* principle, for example, by *Schack*, 'Internationales Zivilverfahrensrecht', 8th edition, C.H. Beck, Munich 2021, p. 14 et seq.

is clarified by the new wording of Art. 18(a) PP. This does not mean that the law applicable under Art. 17 and 17a PP has no implications for procedure. For example, the (potentially foreign) *lex causae* decides whether and to which extent fatherhood can only be challenged by a final court decision;[30] the *lex fori* then governs the procedure leading to this decision and how it has to be conducted.

Authentic instruments: binding legal effects and evidentiary effects not part of the law applicable to parenthood – deletion of Art. 18(b) PP

94) The current Art. 18(b) PP provides that the binding legal effects and evidentiary effects of authentic instruments shall be governed by the law applicable to parenthood. Traditionally, the effects of authentic instruments (unlike presumptions of law and burden of proof, see below para. 96) are characterised as procedural issues subject to the *lex fori* of the State under whose procedural law the authentic instrument was set up. There is no reason to deviate from this general approach in the area of parenthood. Furthermore, the Parenthood Proposal is slightly contradictory here. Art. 35 et seq. PP and Art. 44 et seq. PP want to extend the binding legal effects and evidentiary effects of authentic instruments from the Member State of origin to other Member States. This presupposes that these effects are governed by the law of the Member State of origin, i.e. the Member State in which the authentic instrument on parenthood was formally drawn up or registered (cf. Art. 4(7) PP), even if that Member State is bound under Art. 17 PP or Art. 17a PP to apply the law of another State to the establishment or termination of parenthood.

Rephrasing of Art. 18(c) PP in the light of the new Art. 18(a) PP

95) The Group proposes rephrasing Art. 18(c) PP to clarify its meaning. Since questions of procedure should be left to the *lex fori* (Art. 18(a) PP), Art. 18(c) PP does not encompass any procedural questions but only covers the substantive right to establish or terminate parenthood.

Presumption of law and burden of proof: a new Art. 18(e) PP

96) The Parenthood Proposal does not clarify that the rules which raise presumptions of law or determine the burden of proof are governed by the law applicable to parenthood. In the area of parenthood, such rules are rather relevant, for example, when biological fatherhood is presumed if the potential father had sexual intercourse with the mother during the period of conception.[31] Hence, as

[30] As laid down, for example, in Section 1599(1) of the German Civil Code.

[31] See, for example, Section 1600d(2) and (3) of the German Civil Code.

Art. 18(1) of the Rome I Regulation and Art. 22(1) of the Rome II Regulation (Council Regulation (EC) 864/2007 of 11 July 2007 on the law applicable to non-contractual obligations [2007] OJ L199/40) do, the future Regulation should clarify that such rules are part of the *lex causae*, defined by Art. 17 and 17a PP.

Clarifying the delineation between questions of formal validity and substantive law: a new Art. 18(f) PP

97) It can be difficult to draw the line between aspects of formal validity, which are covered by Art. 20 PP, and aspects of substantive law, which are governed by the law determined by Art. 17 and 17a PP.[32] In the present context, this is especially true for the question of to whom an act establishing or terminating parenthood must be addressed. It would be helpful and lead to more legal certainty if this question was not left to interpretation but directly addressed in a new Art. 18(f) PP. The Group is of the opinion that it is more appropriate to consider this aspect to be part of substantive law. This is because the question of which person or authority a declaration must be addressed to is closely linked to the other material conditions which must be fulfilled in order for a declaration in matters of parenthood to be deemed valid under a certain national law.

Article 18a
Adoption

In matters of adoption, the courts competent under Chapter II *shall apply the law of the forum. In all other cases, adoption shall be governed by the law of the country in which the person to be adopted has his or her habitual residence at the time of adoption.*

Comments

98) The Parenthood Proposal seems to be based on the misconception that all adoptions that are not intercountry adoptions within the meaning of the Hague Adoption Convention are (purely) domestic adoptions. This is not the case (see below para. 99). The Group, therefore, proposes a special conflict rule for adoption, which should not be subject to the general rules in Art. 17 and 17a PP.

---

[32] See, for example, in the context of the Succession Regulation, CJEU 2 June 2022, Case C-617/20 (*T.N. and N.N.*), ECLI:EU:C:2022:426.

Certain kinds of adoption within the scope of the Parenthood Proposal

99) Art. 3(2)(e) PP excludes intercountry adoptions in the sense of the Hague Adoption Convention from the scope of the proposed Regulation. This exclusion does not mean, however, that only purely domestic adoptions that never raise questions of international jurisdiction or applicable law fall within the scope of the Parenthood Proposal. For example, the adoption of a Spanish child who is habitually resident in Germany by two German nationals habitually resident in Germany decreed by a German Court does not fall within the scope of the Hague Adoption Convention and therefore is not an 'intercountry adoption'. Nevertheless, it is a cross-border case (because of the Spanish nationality of the child). Therefore, Chapter II on jurisdiction and Chapter III on applicable law would apply to these adoptions.

100) One has to differentiate between three different categories of adoption:

> (1) Intercountry adoptions within the meaning of the Hague Adoption Convention: they are excluded from the scope of the Parenthood Proposal (Art. 3(2)(e) PP).
>
> (2) Domestic adoptions with an international element (usually because of the foreign nationality of the adoptive child or the adoptive parents): they fall within the scope of the Parenthood Proposal according to Art. 1 and 3(1) PP and raise questions of jurisdiction and applicable law. The Group proposes to introduce a specific conflict rule for them (see below para. 101).
>
> (3) Purely domestic adoptions with no international element: they do not raise questions of jurisdiction and applicable law, but if they are issued by a Member State court (or similar authority), they can be recognised under Chapter IV.

The primary conflict rule: lex fori approach in case of adoption in a Member State

101) Domestic adoptions with an international element (see above para. 100) should not be covered by the general conflict rule of Art. 17 PP. The easiest and most convenient solution would be to explicitly state in a new Art. 18a PP that the courts in each Member State can apply their own law when issuing an adoption. This solution is justified because, in the case of adoption, the applicable law is not decisive for the international recognition of adoptions; the only issue which lies at the heart of adoption (of minors) is the best interests of the child. This is why the Hague Adoption Convention does not contain any rules on the applicable law. The success of this Convention, which 101 States have ratified so far, ensures the international recognition of adoptions and is evidence that foreign States are regularly willing to recognise adoptions – irrespective of the law applied – as long as the best interests of the child have been carefully assessed.

102) Already under current law, all Member States must make sure that the best interests of the child are respected when their courts decree an adoption (cf. *inter alia* Art. 21 of the United Nations Convention on the Rights of the Child (UNCRC), Art. 8 of the European Convention on Human Rights (ECHR) and the jurisprudence of the European Court of Human Rights (ECtHR) on this matter,[33] as well as the European Convention on the Adoption of Children, which is in force in Belgium, Denmark, Finland, Germany, Malta, the Netherlands, Romania and Spain). Since adoptions in all Member States are always issued by courts, any cross-border effects of an adoption are based on the recognition of the court decision. According to the Parenthood Proposal, the rules applicable to the recognition include a public policy exception in Art. 31(1)(a) PP, which would suffice as a safeguard against decisions from Member States which do not adequately take the best interests of the child into account.

Habitual residence for private adoptions in third States

103) Adoptions in countries outside the European Union typically do not fall within the scope of the Parenthood Proposal. Usually, those adoptions are issued by court decree; therefore, each Member State's national recognition laws apply. In rare cases, the validity of a 'private' adoption in a third State (i.e. an adoption not issued by a court or a similar authority) has to be assessed from the point of view of the Member States. This assessment depends on the applicable law, and therefore, there should be uniform rules within the European Union to decide which law is governing the validity of such a private adoption. Art. 18a PP in sentence 2 proposes to apply the law of the habitual residence of the child in order to determine the validity of such an adoption. This is the law which is most closely connected to the situation. In many cases, private adoptions also raise serious public policy questions (Art. 22 PP) because the child's best interests are often not sufficiently protected.

Article 19
Change of applicable law

Where parenthood has been established in a Member State pursuant to this Regulation, a subsequent change of the applicable law shall not affect the parenthood already established.

Where parenthood has been established ~~in a Member State~~ pursuant to this Regulation, a subsequent change of the applicable law shall not affect the parenthood already established.

[33] ECtHR 28 June 2007, Case 76240/01 (*Wagner/Luxembourg*), para. 133.

Comments

104) The Group welcomes that the Parenthood Proposal suggests an explicit rule on the change of the applicable law to parenthood – a rule missing in some Member States so far. The need for such a rule is evident: in particular, the law determined by Art. 17(2) PP can change even after parenthood has been established, for example, if the child relocates his or her habitual residence.

Clarification regarding the protection of vested rights

105) Art. 19 PP wants to ensure that parenthood which was validly established according to the law applicable under Art. 17 PP subsists when a connecting factor changes (e.g. habitual residence of the child under the new Art. 17(2) PP). This principle will be more clearly expressed if the term 'in a Member State' is deleted.

106) The proposed amendment is not intended to be a material change but an attempt to avoid problems of interpretation. The term 'parenthood … established in a Member State' is misleading. Often, one cannot localise a particular Member State where parenthood is established. If a woman gives birth to a child, all Member States will regard this person as the child's legal mother. Parenthood is a universally accepted legal relationship that automatically takes effect when certain conditions are fulfilled. The question of whether parenthood is registered, for example, in a birth register is – apart from rare cases – of no material importance.

Article 20
Formal validity

1. A unilateral act intended to have legal effect on the establishment of parenthood shall be valid as to form where it meets the requirements of one of the following laws:	1. A*ny* ~~unilateral~~ act intended to have legal effect on the establishment of parenthood shall be valid as to form where it meets the requirements of one of the following laws:
(a) the law applicable to the establishment of parenthood pursuant to Article 17;	
(b) the law of the State in which the person doing the act has the habitual residence; or	
(c) the law of the State in which the act was done.	

2. An act intended to have legal effect on the establishment of parenthood may be proved by any mode of proof recognised by the law of the forum or by any of the laws referred to in paragraph 1 under which that act is formally valid, provided that such mode of proof can be administered by the forum.	~~2. An act intended to have legal effect on the establishment of parenthood may be proved by any mode of proof recognised by the law of the forum or by any of the laws referred to in paragraph 1 under which that act is formally valid, provided that such mode of proof can be administered by the forum.~~

Comments

Provision on formal validity should cover multilateral declarations and leave questions of proof to the lex fori

107) The new wording of paragraph 1 of Art. 20 PP is only a clarification. Acts intended to have a legal effect on the establishment of parenthood are, indeed, usually 'unilateral' (e.g. the recognition of parenthood). Still, in some cases, these acts might also be based on the consensus of two or more parties (e.g. surrogacy agreements).

108) The second paragraph of Art. 20 PP should be deleted. Questions of proof are generally not covered by European Regulations; these questions are better left to the *lex fori.*

Article 21
Exclusion of renvoi

The application of the law of any State specified by this Regulation means the application of the rules of law in force in that State other than its rules of private international law.

Article 22
Public policy (ordre public)

1. The application of a provision of the law of any State specified by this Regulation may be refused only if such application is manifestly incompatible with the public policy (ordre public) of the forum.

2. Paragraph 1 shall be applied by the courts and other competent authorities of the Member States in observance of the fundamental rights and principles laid down in the Charter, in particular Article 21 thereof on the right to non-discrimination.

Article 22a
Overriding mandatory provisions

1. Overriding mandatory provisions are provisions the respect for which is regarded as crucial by a country for safeguarding its public interests, such as its social and political organisation, to such an extent that they are applicable to any situation falling within their scope, irrespective of the law otherwise applicable to parenthood under this Regulation.

2. Nothing in this Regulation shall restrict the application of the overriding mandatory provisions of the law of the forum.

Comments

Need for a provision on overriding mandatory provisions: a new Art. 22a PP

109) A rule on overriding mandatory provisions is not a necessary part of the *acquis communautaire*. Some of the Regulations in the area of family and succession law contain such a provision (cf. Art. 30 of the Succession Regulation and Art. 30 of the Property Regulations for spouses and registered partners); others do not (cf. the Rome III Regulation and the Maintenance Regulation). In the context of the Parenthood Proposal, a similar provision seems to be advisable. It could, for example, cover national rules on abusive acknowledgments of paternity which do not correspond to a genuine parental connection but rather are aimed at creating residence or nationality rights, such as Section 1597a of the German Civil Code. Art. 22a PP must, of course, be interpreted in the light of the Charter of Fundamental Rights and, in particular, Art. 21 thereof, which prohibits discrimination.

Article 23
States with more than one legal system

1. Where the law specified by this Regulation is that of a State which comprises several territorial units each of which has its own rules of law in respect of parenthood matters, the internal conflict-of-laws rules of that State shall determine the relevant territorial unit whose rules of law are to apply.

2. In the absence of such internal conflict-of-laws rules:

(a) any reference to the law of the State referred to in paragraph 1 shall, for the purposes of determining the law applicable pursuant to the provision referring to the habitual residence of the person giving birth at the time of birth, be construed as referring to the law of the territorial unit in which the person giving birth has the habitual residence;

(b) any reference to the law of the State referred to in paragraph 1 shall, for the purposes of determining the law applicable pursuant to the provisions referring to the State of birth of the child, be construed as referring to the law of the territorial unit where the child was born.

(c) A Member State which comprises several territorial units each of which has its own rules of law in respect of parenthood matters shall not be required to apply this Regulation to conflicts of laws arising between such units only.

CHAPTER IV
RECOGNITION

SECTION 1
General provisions on recognition

Article 24
Recognition of a court decision

1. A court decision on parenthood given in a Member State shall be recognised in all other Member States without any special procedure being required.	
2. In particular, no special procedure shall be required for updating the civil-status records of a Member State on the basis of a court decision on parenthood given in another Member State and against which no further appeal lies under the law of that Member State.	2. In particular, *and without prejudice to Article 25 and Article 32*, no special procedure shall be required for updating the civil-status records of a Member State on the basis of a court decision on parenthood given in another Member State and against which no further appeal lies under the law of that Member State.
3. Where the recognition of a court decision is raised as an incidental question before a court of a Member State, that court may determine that issue.	3. Where the recognition of a court decision is raised as an incidental question before a court *or other competent authority* of *another* Member State, that court *or authority* may determine that issue.

Comments

110) Art. 24(1) PP states in a familiar manner that a court decision on parenthood given in another Member State shall be recognised in all other Member States without the need for a special formal procedure.

111) Art. 24(2) PP deals with the updating of civil status records requested in a Member State on the basis of a foreign parenthood decision. Unlike Art. 30(2) of the Brussels IIb Regulation ('without prejudice to'), Art. 24(2) PP does not contain a reservation in favour of the special recognition procedure in Art. 25 PP. Nevertheless, a registrar should refrain from deciding to update the register

entry if proceedings under Art. 25 PP are pending and should await the outcome of these proceedings.[34] He or she should proceed in the same way if proceedings for refusal of recognition under Art. 32 PP are pending.[35] The Group's proposed amendments would clarify this.

112) Art. 24(3) PP governs the recognition of a court decision on parenthood given in another Member State when it arises as an incidental question. The provision corresponds to Art. 30(5) of the Brussels IIb Regulation. The recognition of a court decision on parenthood can, however, be raised as an incidental question not only before a court (in the sense of Art. 4(4) PP), but also before all other authorities of a Member State, especially civil status registrars (e.g. when he or she is requested to register a name if parenthood is an incidental question). Even if there is agreement with regard to comparable provisions in other European Regulations that the limitation to court proceedings does not exclude an incidental review of the recognition issue in other administrative proceedings,[36] this point should be clarified. Therefore, the Group proposes that Art. 24(3) PP is extended to all competent authorities of a Member State.

Article 25
Decision that there are no grounds for refusal of recognition

1. Any interested party may, in accordance with the procedures provided for in Articles 32 to 34, apply for a decision that there are no grounds for refusal of recognition referred to in Article 31.

2. The local jurisdiction of the court communicated to the Commission pursuant to Article 71 shall be determined by the law of the Member State in which proceedings in accordance with paragraph 1 are brought.

---

[34] cf. *Hau*, in Staudinger, 'Bürgerliches Gesetzbuch', de Gruyter, Berlin, 2023, Art. 30 Brussels IIb Regulation para. 30.

[35] cf. *Hau*, in Staudinger, 'Bürgerliches Gesetzbuch', 2023, Art. 30 Brussels IIb Regulation para. 30.

[36] *Hau*, in Staudinger, 'Bürgerliches Gesetzbuch', 2023, Art. 30 Brussels IIb Regulation para. 44; *Gottwald*, in 'Münchener Kommentar zum FamFG', 3rd edition, C.H. Beck, Munich, 2019, Art. 21 Brussels IIa Regulation para. 15; *Rauscher*, in Rauscher, 'Europäisches Zivilprozess- und Kollisionsrecht', 4th edition, Otto Schmidt, Cologne, 2015, Art. 21 Brussels IIa Regulation para. 30.

Comments

113) Art. 25 PP opens the possibility for parties to apply for a court decision in a special (optional) procedure, which determines whether there are any grounds for refusing the recognition of a decision. This way, the parties can gain a binding declaration on whether – *e contrario* – a decision is to be recognised. The provision corresponds in substance to Art. 30(3) and (4) of the Brussels IIb Regulation. Similar in content are Art. 23(2) of the Maintenance Regulation, Art. 36(2) of the Property Regulations for spouses and registered partners, Art. 39(2) of the Succession Regulation and Art. 36(2) of the Brussels Ia Regulation.

Article 26
Documents to be produced for recognition

1. A party who wishes to invoke in a Member State a court decision given in another Member State shall produce the following:

    (a) a copy of the court decision that satisfies the conditions necessary to establish its authenticity; and

    (b) the appropriate attestation issued pursuant to Article 29.

2. The court or other competent authority before which a court decision given in another Member State is invoked may, where necessary, require the party invoking it to provide a translation or transliteration of the translatable content of the free text fields of the attestation referred to in point (b) of paragraph 1 of this Article.

3. The court or other competent authority before which a court decision given in another Member State is invoked may require the party to provide a translation or transliteration of the court decision in addition to a translation or transliteration of the translatable content of the free text fields of the attestation if it is unable to proceed without such a translation or transliteration.

Comments

114) According to Art. 26(1) PP, a party who wishes to invoke in a Member State a court decision on parenthood given in another Member State shall produce: (a) a copy of the court decision that satisfies the conditions necessary to establish its authenticity; and (b) the appropriate attestation issued pursuant to Art. 29 PP. This provision is consistent with comparable provisions in other Regulations, especially Art. 31 of the Brussels IIb Regulation. The documents to be submitted serve to clarify the existence, the content and the eligibility for recognition of the foreign decision.

115) From a practical point of view, however, the Group questions whether the obligation to present both documents in every case is reasonable. The attestation pursuant to Art. 29 PP not only indicates which persons are the child's parents (with all the necessary identifying information), but also the necessary information for some of the grounds to refuse recognition or to stay the proceedings. In particular, the attestation shall state whether the decision was issued by default (cf. Art. 31(1)(b) PP) and whether the decision is subject to further appeal under the law of the Member State of origin (cf. Art. 28(a) PP). In view of all this information apparent from the attestation, it is unclear what additional information the submission of a certified copy of the court decision is supposed to provide for the court or other competent authority of the Member State in which recognition is sought. In many cases, the court or other competent authority of the Member State in which recognition is sought will not be able to avoid a translation of the court decision (cf. Art. 26(3) PP) if it has to verify the content of the decision independently and cannot rely solely on the attestation.

> **Example**: If the paternity of a man is established in a Greek court decision, a German civil status officer will not be able to read the original court decision simply because of the Greek script. A time-consuming and costly certified translation is unavoidable. In such cases, the attestations do not make the recognition procedure easier and faster.

116) Generally, it does not appear to be necessary to always provide both a certified copy of the court decision and the attestation. Therefore, the Commission should consider whether the submission of a copy of the court decision should be limited to cases of doubt. In such cases, the competent authority before which a court decision given in another Member State is invoked may require the party to provide a certified copy of the court decision and a translation or transliteration.

Article 27
Absence of documents

1. If the documents specified in Article 26(1) are not produced, the court or other competent authority before which a court decision given in another Member State is invoked may specify a time for its production, accept equivalent documents or, if it considers that it has sufficient information before it, dispense with its production.

2. If the court or other competent authority before which a court decision given in another Member State is invoked so requires, a translation or transliteration of such equivalent documents shall be produced.

Comments

117) Art. 27 PP corresponds to Art. 32 of the Brussels IIb Regulation.

Article 28
Stay of proceedings

The court before which a court decision given in another Member State is invoked may stay its proceedings, in whole or in part, where:

(a) an ordinary appeal against that court decision has been lodged in the Member State of origin; or

(b) an application has been submitted for a decision that there are no grounds for refusal of recognition referred to in Article 25 or for a decision that the recognition is to be refused on the basis of one of those grounds.

(b) an application has been submitted for a decision that there are no grounds for refusal of recognition referred to in Article ~~25~~ *31* or for a decision that the recognition is to be refused on the basis of one of those grounds.

Comments

118) Art. 28 PP corresponds to Art. 33 of the Brussels IIb Regulation.

119) The proposed amendment of Art. 28(b) PP corrects a drafting error.

Article 29
Issuance of the attestation

1. The court of a Member State of origin as communicated to the Commission pursuant to Article 71 shall, upon application by a party, issue an attestation for a court decision on parenthood using the form set out in Annex I.

2. The attestation shall be completed and issued in the language of the court decision. The attestation may also be issued in another official language of the institutions of the European Union requested by the party. This does not create any obligation for the court issuing the attestation to provide a translation or transliteration of the translatable content of the free text fields.

3. The attestation shall contain a statement informing Union citizens and their family members that the attestation does not affect the rights that a child derives from Union law and that, for the exercise of such rights, proof of the parent-child relationship can be presented by any means.

4. No challenge shall lie against the issuance of the attestation

Comments

120) Art. 29 PP corresponds to Art. 36 of the Brussels IIb Regulation. While the European legislator speaks of 'certificate' there, it calls the forms 'attestation' here. A new paragraph 3 has been added, which has no precedent in the European Regulations, and which does no harm but little good.

Article 30
Rectification of the attestation

1. The court of a Member State of origin as communicated to the Commission pursuant to Article 71 shall, upon application, and may, of its own motion, rectify the attestation where, due to a material error or omission, there is a discrepancy between the court decision to be recognised and the attestation.

2. The law of the Member State of origin shall apply to the procedure for rectification of the attestation.

Comments

121) Art. 30 PP corresponds to Art. 37 of the Brussels IIb Regulation.

Article 31
Grounds for refusal of recognition

1. The recognition of a court decision shall be refused:	1. The recognition of a court decision *on parenthood given in a Member State* shall be refused:
(a) if such recognition is manifestly contrary to the public policy of the Member State in which recognition is invoked, taking into account the child's interests;	(a) if such recognition is manifestly contrary to the public policy of the Member State in which recognition is invoked~~, taking into account the child's interests~~;
(b) where it was given in default of appearance if the persons in default were not served with the document which instituted the proceedings or with an equivalent document in sufficient time and in such a way as to enable those persons to arrange for their defence unless it is determined that such persons have accepted the court decision unequivocally;	
(c) upon application by any person claiming that the court decision infringes his fatherhood or her motherhood over the child if it was given without such person having been given an opportunity to be heard;	(c) upon application by any person claiming that the court decision infringes ~~his fatherhood or her motherhood~~ *his or her parenthood* over the child if it was given without such person having been given an opportunity to be heard;
(d) if and to the extent that it is irreconcilable with a later court decision relating to parenthood given in the Member State in which recognition is invoked;	(d) if and to the extent that it is irreconcilable with a ~~later~~ court decision relating to parenthood given in the Member State in which recognition is invoked;

(e) if and to the extent that it is irreconcilable with a later court decision relating to parenthood given in another Member State provided that the later court decision fulfils the conditions necessary for its recognition in the Member State in which recognition is invoked.

(e) if and to the extent that it is irreconcilable with *an* ~~later~~ *earlier* court decision relating to parenthood given in another Member State, provided that the ~~later~~ *earlier* court decision fulfils the conditions necessary for its recognition in the Member State in which recognition is invoked.

2. Point (a) of paragraph 1 shall be applied by the courts and other competent authorities of the Member States in observance of the fundamental rights and principles laid down in the Charter, in particular Article 21 thereof on the right to non-discrimination.

3. The recognition of a court decision in matters of parenthood may be refused if it was given without children having been given an opportunity to express their views, unless this is against the interest of the child. Where children were below the age of 18 years, this provision shall apply where the children were capable of forming their views in accordance with Article 15.

~~3. The recognition of a court decision in matters of parenthood may be refused if it was given without children having been given an opportunity to express their views, unless this is against the interest of the child. Where children were below the age of 18 years, this provision shall apply where the children were capable of forming their views in accordance with Article 15.~~

Comments

122) The Group notes that Art. 31 PP mainly builds on Art. 39 of the Brussels IIb Regulation, which lists the grounds for non-recognition of a decision in matters of parental responsibility.

123) This blind transfer fails to recognise that decisions on the establishment or termination of parenthood differ in many respects from decisions on matters of parental responsibility. Therefore, the Group is of the opinion that some amendments are necessary.

Violation of public policy, Art. 31(1)(a) PP

124) In principle, the public policy reservation as a reason for refusal of recognition in Art. 31(1)(a) PP is convincing. However, its wording should not exceed the wording used in many other Regulations (e.g. Art. 38(a) of the Brussels IIb Regulation; Art. 40(a) of the Succession Regulation). The best interests of the child should not be explicitly highlighted as a relevant aspect, as the wording (apparently taken from Art. 39(a) of the Brussels IIb Regulation) can be misleading and even interpreted to the detriment of the child.

125) It is, of course, true that the child's best interests must be a primary consideration when it comes to the question of whether the recognition of a court decision given in a Member State establishing or terminating parenthood may or may not be refused. This consideration already follows from Art. 24 of the Charter of Fundamental Rights. Moreover, Art. 31(2) PP expressly emphasises that recognising a judicial decision may not be refused on the grounds of public policy if this violates the fundamental rights and principles laid down in the Charter, in particular the right to non-discrimination (Art. 21 of the Charter).[37]

126) In order to address this legitimate concern, the Group recommends a Recital explicitly emphasising that the child's best interests must be a primary consideration under the public policy exception. There, the wording can clarify that family relationships *established* in a court decision of a Member State may not be refused recognition solely because they are based on a special family relationship (e.g. same-sex parenthood or parenthood of intended parents after surrogacy). Such a Recital can provide clarity for legal practice as to which aspects, in particular, are considered discriminatory from the perspective of the European legislator and therefore must not be used as a basis for applying the public policy exception.

127) The current reference to the best interests of the child could lead courts or other competent authorities in the State of recognition to not recognise a court decision on parenthood given in another Member State on substantive grounds. For example, a recognising authority could argue that a court decision on parenthood is not compatible with the best interests of the child because the parenthood established therein does not correspond to biological parenthood or because another person is more likely to be a biological parent. Such new substantive considerations are, however, inadmissible in the recognition procedure. Furthermore, court decisions of another Member State must be recognised even if the decision removes one parent, e.g. as a result of a contestation of paternity. The fact that the child loses a legal parent and suffers

[37] See also Recital 75.

both personal and economic disadvantages might not be in the child's best interests. Nonetheless, this aspect will usually not justify refusal of recognition of such a decision. Recognition can even be necessary in order for another person to be able to establish his or her parenthood for the benefit of the child.

Lack of hearing, Art. 31(1)(c) PP

128) The provision intends to protect the generally accepted principle of the right to be heard; this is a special form of procedural public policy.

129) The Group is of the opinion that a ground for refusal of recognition is only justified if the court decision which is to be recognised infringes on the applicant's *legal* parenthood. Consequently, the legal definition in Art. 4(1) PP should be used here instead of the less precise term 'his fatherhood or her motherhood'.

130) This clarification removes the ambiguity as to whether a putative biological father can also invoke this ground for refusal of recognition. This has to be excluded. If a putative biological father could also prevent the recognition of a court decision on legal parenthood merely by claiming that the decision affects his biological parenthood, the free movement of court decisions on parenthood given in a Member State would be prevented in many cases. A putative biological father who wants to be a legal father must raise all substantive issues in the proceedings in the Member State of origin; they cannot be considered in the recognition proceedings.

Irreconcilability with a court decision from the recognising State, Art. 31(1)(d) PP

131) The wording of Art. 31(1)(d) PP was copied from Art. 39(1)(d) of the Brussels IIb Regulation without taking into account the specifics of the context in question.

132) The amendments proposed by the Group consider the well-known and established fact in European recognition law that more trust is, and may be placed, in a court decision from the recognising State than in a court decision from another Member State (cf. e.g. Art. 38(c) of the Brussels IIb Regulation). This applies even if the recognising State's court has disregarded the *lis pendens* rule (Art. 14 PP).[38] However, the reason for greater reliance on one's own court decisions applies even more to court decisions that were issued before the foreign decision whose recognition is now sought. For this reason, the Group suggests deleting the word 'later'.

---

[38] cf. Recital 63.

133) When assessing whether a decision cannot be recognised because it is irreconcilable with another decision, particular caution is required. First of all, it must be noted that recognition can only be refused to those decisions that relate to the same parenthood position as addressed in the domestic decision. However, when assessing a possible conflict, it must also be remembered that parenthood may change in the course of time. Therefore, e.g. as a result of a paternity contestation, different court decisions may be issued on the same parenthood which are not irreconcilable with each other within the meaning of Art. 31(1)(d) PP (e.g. contestation of A's paternity in one Member State and subsequent establishment of B as the father by judicial determination in another Member State).

Irreconcilability with a court decision from a Member State or third State, Art. 31(1)(e) PP

134) The provision in Art. 31(1)(e) PP, which gives priority to the later of different foreign court decisions and declares an obstacle to recognition for the earlier one, is obviously copied from Art. 39(1)(e) of the Brussels IIb Regulation.

135) The Group urges the European legislator to reconsider this provision. In the Brussels IIb Regulation, the relevant provision, which deviates from the normal *res iudicata* rule, applies only to matters of parental responsibility (and not to matrimonial matters, cf. Art. 38(d) of the Brussels IIb Regulation), i.e. only to matters of custody and rights of access. In these areas, the provision can be justified by the fact that it is always possible to amend judgments issued on parental custody or rights of access if circumstances have changed.[39] Art. 39(1)(e) of the Brussels IIb Regulation accounts for this by stipulating that the most recent decision (which is based on the current circumstances) should prevail: if the domestic custody decision is the most recent, it supersedes an earlier foreign custody decision and prevents its recognition. However, this ratio of the special rule for cases of parental responsibility cannot be applied to status proceedings such as cases of parenthood. Court decisions on parenthood are primarily based on unchangeable circumstances at the time of birth or on one-off declarations (such as an acknowledgment of paternity); for this reason, court decisions on parenthood are usually endowed with increased legal force: they apply not only *inter partes* but even *erga omnes* vis-à-vis all third parties and the State. Should the Commission have had in mind decisions on a contestation of an existing legal parenthood, it should be noted that such challenges are regularly only possible if the parenthood to be contested was not established in a prior court decision, but

[39] *Lazić*, in Magnus/Mankowski, 'European Commentaries on Private International Law', de Gruyter, Berlin, 2023, Art. 39 Brussels IIb Regulation para. 16.

rather by operation of law or prior declarations of the parties. Competing court decisions – where Art. 31(1)(e) PP would become relevant – do not arise here. Therefore, the normal *res iudicata* rule must apply, according to which a later court decision cannot be recognised if it is incompatible with an earlier one.

136) This is not contradicted by the fact that there may be cases in which two successive court decisions concerning the same parenthood can be recognised. If the mother or the intended father has first obtained a court decision in which the validity of an acknowledgment of paternity is (legally) established, its legal force does not prevent a later court decision in which the same paternity is terminated after a challenge to paternity, since there is no 'irreconcilability' due to different facts and other parties involved.[40] In this case, too, not only the later court decision must be recognised, but both decisions must be recognised, with the consequence that the parenthood in question is terminated due to the challenge.

Failure to hear the child, Art. 31(3) PP

137) The provision corresponds to Art. 39(2) of the Brussels IIb Regulation,[41] but does not fit for decisions on parenthood that concern the status relationship.

138) Court decisions on parenthood are predominantly based on the biological parenthood of the child (see above para. 59 et seq.); as such, a hearing of the child is not necessary. A hearing could, at most, become relevant in parenthood proceedings in which biological descent is not important or not decisive, such as in adoption proceedings in particular. However, the adoption procedure is, in any case, determined solely by the best interests of the child and usually even requires the consent of the child, who may be represented by a legal representative if he or she is not (yet) able to express his or her own opinion. In the case of an acknowledgment of paternity, it also may be the case that the legal parenthood of the child is established irrespective of the biological parenthood. In these cases, too, the interests of the child will generally be safeguarded by consent requirements in the applicable law so that a separate hearing of the child in the court proceedings does not appear necessary and the lack of such a hearing should not constitute a ground for refusing recognition of the court decision. The Group is of the opinion that those situations, in which a hearing of the child (or his or her participation in another form) may be required under the applicable law but has not taken place, can be addressed and adequately dealt

---

[40] cf. to the terminology, *Lazić*, in Magnus/Mankowski, 'European Commentaries on Private International Law', 2023, Art. 38 Brussels IIb Regulation para. 60 with reference to CJEU rulings.

[41] cf. *Válková*, 'The Commission Proposal for a Regulation on the Recognition of Parenthood and other Legislative Trends affecting Legal Parenthood' in Rivista di diritto internazionale privato e processuale 2023, 854, 894.

with by the general public policy reservation under Art. 31(1)(a) PP.[42] Should the European legislator deem clarification necessary, a separate Recital covering these aspects could be inserted.

139) Since, in principle, no child hearing is required in matters of parenthood (see above para. 59 et seq.), unlike in matters of parental responsibility (cf. Art. 39(2) of the Brussels IIb Regulation), the Group proposes to delete Art. 31(3) PP.

SECTION 2
Procedure for refusal of recognition

Article 32
Application for refusal of recognition

1. The procedure for making an application for refusal of recognition shall, in so far as it is not covered by this Regulation, be governed by the law of the Member State in which proceedings for non-recognition are brought.

2. The recognition of a court decision in matters of parenthood shall be refused if one of the grounds for refusal of recognition referred to in Article 31 is found to exist.

3. The local jurisdiction of the court communicated to the Commission pursuant to Article 71 shall be determined by the law of the Member State in which proceedings for non-recognition are brought.

4. The applicant shall provide the court with a copy of the court decision and, where applicable and possible, the appropriate attestation issued pursuant to Article 29.

---

42 Similar considerations already on the Brussels IIb Regulation, *Lazić et al.*, in Lazić (ed.), 'Recommendations to Improve the Rules on Jurisdiction and on the Enforcement of Decisions in Matrimonial Matters and Matters of Parental Responsibility in the European Union', p. 31, available at www.asser.nl/media/4662/m-5796-ec-justice-cross-border-proceedings-in-family-law-matters-10-publications-00-publications-on-asser-website-recommendations.pdf (last accessed 15 January 2024).

5. The court may, where necessary, require the applicant to provide a translation or transliteration of the translatable content of the free text fields of the appropriate attestation issued pursuant to Article 29.

6. If the court is unable to proceed without a translation or transliteration of the court decision, it may require the applicant to provide such a translation or transliteration.

7. The court may dispense with the production of the documents referred to in paragraph 4 if:

(a) it already possesses them; or

(b) it considers it unreasonable to require the applicant to provide them.

8. The party seeking the refusal of the recognition of a court decision given in another Member State shall not be required to have a postal address in the Member State in which proceedings for non-recognition are brought. That party shall be required to have an authorised representative in the Member State in which proceedings for non-recognition are brought only if such a representative is mandatory under the law of the Member State in which proceedings for non-recognition are brought irrespective of the nationality of the parties.

Comments

140) Art. 32(1), (4) to (8) PP corresponds to Art. 40(1) in connection with Art. 59 of the Brussels IIb Regulation. Art. 32(3) PP corresponds to Art. 40(2) of the Brussels IIb Regulation. Art. 32(2) PP emphasises the standard of review.

Article 33
Challenge or appeal

1. Any party may challenge or appeal against a court decision on the application for refusal of recognition.

2. The challenge or appeal shall be lodged with the court communicated by the Member States to the Commission pursuant to Article 71 as the court with which such a challenge or appeal is to be lodged.

Comments

141) Art. 33 PP corresponds to Art. 40(1) in connection with Art. 61 of the Brussels IIb Regulation.

Article 34
Further challenge or appeal

A court decision given on the challenge or appeal may only be contested by a challenge or appeal where the courts with which any further challenge or appeal is to be lodged have been communicated by the Member State concerned to the Commission pursuant to Article 71.

Comments

142) Art. 34 PP corresponds to Art. 40(1) in connection with Art. 62 of the Brussels IIb Regulation.

SECTION 3
Authentic instruments with binding legal effect

Article 35
Scope

This Section shall apply to authentic instruments establishing parenthood that:

(a) have been formally drawn up or registered in a Member State assuming jurisdiction under Chapter II; and

(b) have binding legal effect in the Member State where they have been formally drawn up or registered.

Article 36
Recognition of authentic instruments

Authentic instruments establishing parenthood with binding legal effect in the Member State of origin shall be recognised in other Member States without any special procedure being required. Sections 1 and 2 of this Chapter shall apply accordingly, unless otherwise provided for in this Section.

Article 37
Attestation

1. The competent authority of the Member State of origin as communicated to the Commission pursuant to Article 71 shall, upon application by a party, issue an attestation for an authentic instrument establishing parenthood with binding legal effect using the form set out in Annex II.

~~**SECTION 3**~~
~~**Authentic instruments with binding legal effect**~~

~~**Article 35**~~
~~**Scope**~~

~~This Section shall apply to authentic instruments establishing parenthood that:~~

~~(a) have been formally drawn up or registered in a Member State assuming jurisdiction under Chapter II; and~~

~~(b) have binding legal effect in the Member State where they have been formally drawn up or registered.~~

~~**Article 36**~~
~~**Recognition of authentic instruments**~~

~~Authentic instruments establishing parenthood with binding legal effect in the Member State of origin shall be recognised in other Member States without any special procedure being required. Sections 1 and 2 of this Chapter shall apply accordingly, unless otherwise provided for in this Section.~~

~~**Article 37**~~
~~**Attestation**~~

~~1. The competent authority of the Member State of origin as communicated to the Commission pursuant to Article 71 shall, upon application by a party, issue an attestation for an authentic instrument establishing parenthood with binding legal effect using the form set out in Annex II.~~

2. The attestation may be issued only if the following conditions are met:	~~2. The attestation may be issued only if the following conditions are met:~~
(a) the Member State which empowered the public authority or other authority to formally draw up or register the authentic instrument establishing parenthood had jurisdiction under Chapter II; and	~~(a) the Member State which empowered the public authority or other authority to formally draw up or register the authentic instrument establishing parenthood had jurisdiction under Chapter II; and~~
(b) the authentic instrument has binding legal effect in that Member State.	~~(b) the authentic instrument has binding legal effect in that Member State.~~
3. The attestation shall be completed in the language of the authentic instrument. It may also be issued in another official language of the institutions of the European Union requested by the party. This does not create any obligation for the competent authority issuing the attestation to provide a translation or transliteration of the translatable content of the free text fields.	~~3. The attestation shall be completed in the language of the authentic instrument. It may also be issued in another official language of the institutions of the European Union requested by the party. This does not create any obligation for the competent authority issuing the attestation to provide a translation or transliteration of the translatable content of the free text fields.~~
4. The attestation shall contain a statement informing Union citizens and their family members that the attestation does not affect the rights that a child derives from Union law and that, for the exercise of such rights, proof of the parent-child relationship can be presented by any means.	~~4. The attestation shall contain a statement informing Union citizens and their family members that the attestation does not affect the rights that a child derives from Union law and that, for the exercise of such rights, proof of the parent-child relationship can be presented by any means.~~
5. If the attestation is not produced, the authentic instrument shall not be recognised in another Member State.	~~5. If the attestation is not produced, the authentic instrument shall not be recognised in another Member State.~~

Article 38 **Rectification and withdrawal of the attestation**	~~**Article 38**~~ ~~**Rectification and withdrawal of the attestation**~~
1. The competent authority of the Member State of origin as communicated to the Commission pursuant to Article 71 shall, upon application, and may, of its own motion, rectify the attestation where, due to a material error or omission, there is a discrepancy between the authentic instrument and the attestation.	~~1. The competent authority of the Member State of origin as communicated to the Commission pursuant to Article 71 shall, upon application, and may, of its own motion, rectify the attestation where, due to a material error or omission, there is a discrepancy between the authentic instrument and the attestation.~~
2. The competent authority referred to in paragraph 1 of this Article shall, upon application or of its own motion, withdraw the attestation where it was wrongly granted, having regard to the requirements laid down in Article 37.	~~2. The competent authority referred to in paragraph 1 of this Article shall, upon application or of its own motion, withdraw the attestation where it was wrongly granted, having regard to the requirements laid down in Article 37.~~
3. The procedure, including any appeal, with regard to the rectification or withdrawal of the attestation shall be governed by the law of the Member State of origin.	~~3. The procedure, including any appeal, with regard to the rectification or withdrawal of the attestation shall be governed by the law of the Member State of origin.~~
Article 39 **Grounds for refusal of recognition**	~~**Article 39**~~ ~~**Grounds for refusal of recognition**~~
1. The recognition of an authentic instrument establishing parenthood with binding legal effect shall be refused:	~~1. The recognition of an authentic instrument establishing parenthood with binding legal effect shall be refused:~~
(a) if such recognition is manifestly contrary to the public policy of the Member State in which recognition is invoked, taking into account the child's interests;	~~(a) if such recognition is manifestly contrary to the public policy of the Member State in which recognition is invoked, taking into account the child's interests;~~

(b) upon application by any person claiming that the authentic instrument infringes his fatherhood or her motherhood over the child, if the authentic instrument was formally drawn up or registered without that person having been involved;	~~(b) upon application by any person claiming that the authentic instrument infringes his fatherhood or her motherhood over the child, if the authentic instrument was formally drawn up or registered without that person having been involved;~~
(c) if and to the extent that it is irreconcilable with a later court decision relating to parenthood given, or a later authentic instrument establishing parenthood with binding legal effect drawn up or registered, in the Member State in which recognition is invoked;	~~(c) if and to the extent that it is irreconcilable with a later court decision relating to parenthood given, or a later authentic instrument establishing parenthood with binding legal effect drawn up or registered, in the Member State in which recognition is invoked;~~
(d) if and to the extent that it is irreconcilable with a later court decision relating to parenthood given, or a later authentic instrument establishing parenthood with binding legal effect drawn up or registered, in another Member State provided that the later court decision or authentic instrument fulfils the conditions necessary for its recognition in the Member State in which recognition is invoked.	~~(d) if and to the extent that it is irreconcilable with a later court decision relating to parenthood given, or a later authentic instrument establishing parenthood with binding legal effect drawn up or registered, in another Member State provided that the later court decision or authentic instrument fulfils the conditions necessary for its recognition in the Member State in which recognition is invoked.~~
2. Point (a) of paragraph 1 shall be applied by the courts and other competent authorities of the Member States in observance of the fundamental rights and principles laid down in the Charter, in particular Article 21 thereof on the right to non-discrimination.	~~2. Point (a) of paragraph 1 shall be applied by the courts and other competent authorities of the Member States in observance of the fundamental rights and principles laid down in the Charter, in particular Article 21 thereof on the right to non-discrimination.~~

3. The recognition of an authentic instrument establishing parenthood with binding legal effect may be refused if it was formally drawn up or registered without children having been given an opportunity to express their views. Where the children were below the age of 18 years, this provision shall apply where the children were capable of forming their views.

~~3. The recognition of an authentic instrument establishing parenthood with binding legal effect may be refused if it was formally drawn up or registered without children having been given an opportunity to express their views. Where the children were below the age of 18 years, this provision shall apply where the children were capable of forming their views.~~

Comments

143) In Art. 35 et seq. PP, the Commission proposes rules on the recognition of authentic instruments (as defined in Art. 4(6) PP) establishing parenthood with binding legal effect in the Member State of origin. Such authentic instruments shall be recognised automatically in the other Member States (see Art. 36 PP) if the instrument was formally drawn up or registered in a Member State having jurisdiction for matters relating to parenthood according to Art. 6 et seq. PP (see Art. 35(a) PP) and if there is no ground for refusal of recognition (see Art. 39 PP). By this, the Parenthood Proposal more or less adopts the provisions in Art. 64 et seq. of the Brussels IIb Regulation.

144) The new rules warrant criticism because – at least according to the wording of Art. 35 PP – they are restricted to authentic instruments *establishing* parenthood with binding legal effect and exclude legally binding instruments which *terminate* parenthood (cf. also below para. 149).

145) More generally, however, the Group is of the opinion that there is no room and need for a special recognition regime for authentic instruments with binding legal effect. Rather the provisions on the recognition of court decisions in Art. 24 et seq. PP and on the acceptance of authentic instruments in Art. 44 and 45 PP suffice and should not be weakened by another regime. Furthermore, authentic instruments establishing parenthood with a binding legal effect that could extend to other Member States are unknown in the Member States.

The recognition of authentic instruments after the CJEU's obiter dictum in the TB case

146) On the one hand, the Court of Justice in its Grand Chamber decision in the *TB* case (cf. already para. 22 above) recently indicated in an *obiter dictum* that private divorces recorded by an Italian civil status officer are not covered

by Art. 64 et seq. of the Brussels IIb Regulation,[43] i.e. the provisions on which Art. 35 et seq. PP are built. Against this background, the delineation between the recognition of decisions and authentic instruments has become increasingly blurred.[44] In particular, it is unclear whether there is any room for provisions on the recognition of authentic instruments if – based on the criteria developed by the Court of Justice in the *TB* case – all authentic instruments with recognisable effects are qualified as decisions anyhow.

147) Taking this into account, the European legislator would have to clarify in a Parenthood Regulation exactly which authentic instruments are recognised as authentic instruments and which as decisions. Providing four (!) different regimes for the cross-border circulation of documents – recognition of decisions, recognition of authentic instruments with binding legal effect, acceptance of authentic instruments, and using the European Certificate of Parenthood – will leave not only most European citizens but also the Member State authorities and courts in confusion. The European legislator should, in a Parenthood Regulation, not copy the deficiencies of the Succession Regulation where it is – ten years after its adoption – still unclear whether national certificates of succession, such as the German *Erbschein*, circulate within the European Union as decisions or authentic instruments.[45] Such deficiencies would be even more problematic in parenthood matters because unlike certificates of succession, European citizens have to deal with their civil status documents on a daily basis, and there is no place for legal uncertainty here.

No need for an additional recognition regime

148) The main reason, on the other hand, which speaks against an additional set of rules such as Art. 35 et seq. PP for the recognition of authentic instruments with binding legal effect, is the fact that so far, the Commission has not been able to present a case for such an additional recognition regime. Even after long consideration, the Group has significant doubts that the types of instruments that could potentially be encompassed by these provisions exist at all in the current laws of the Member States.

---

[43] CJEU 15 November 2022, Case C-646/20 (*Senatsverwaltung für Inneres und Sport, Standesamtsaufsicht v. TB*), ECLI:EU:C:2022:879, para. 58 et seq.

[44] See, for example, *Dutta*, 'Mitgliedstaatliche Privatscheidungen vor dem EuGH: Was bleibt nach TB vom neuen Art. 65 Abs. 1 Brüssel IIb-VO?' in Zeitschrift für das gesamte Familienrecht 2023, 16, 17 et seq., and *Mayer*, 'Verfahrensrechtliche Anerkennung der Privatscheidung durch den italienischen Standesbeamten als "gerichtliche Entscheidung"?' in Zeitschrift für Europäisches Privatrecht 2023, 455.

[45] See on the characterisation of national certificates, for example, *Dutta*, in 'Münchener Kommentar zum Bürgerlichen Gesetzbuch', 8th edition, C.H. Beck, Munich, 2020, Art. 3 EuErbVO para. 17.

149) In all Member States of the European Union, parenthood is established by the operation of law (for example, motherhood by birth of the child, fatherhood by marriage with the mother), by private declarations of the parties (fatherhood by acknowledgment) or by a court decision (fatherhood established in court proceedings). The same applies to the termination of parenthood, which mostly requires a court decision (for example, contesting fatherhood) or in exceptional cases declarations of the persons involved (see above para. 87).

150) In light of this, parenthood is often the object of an authentic instrument in the sense of Art. 4(6) PP, for example, in a birth certificate or a document containing the private declarations of the parties. However, those authentic instruments, as such, have no binding legal effects as to the substance of parenthood (which is based, as mentioned, on the operation of law, private declarations or court decisions as provided by the law determined in Art. 17 and 17a PP). For example, if a person recognises fatherhood of a child, this private declaration – even if contained in an authentic instrument – has no binding legal effects which could be recognised in the other Member States according to Art. 35 et seq. PP. Fatherhood is only attributed to the recognising person if, under the law applicable according to Art. 17 PP, all legal conditions for a fatherhood of the recognising person are met, for example, that there is no (statutory) fatherhood of another person barring the fatherhood of the recognising person, or the mother or the child consented to the recognition of fatherhood. All those legal consequences of the private declarations flow from the applicable law and not from the authentic instrument containing the private declaration. Thus, the private declaration is only one element for the establishment of fatherhood under the governing law (which has also to be applied by the other Member States and their authorities). Rather, authentic instruments on parenthood have only evidentiary effects, for example, regarding the fact that the person has acknowledged fatherhood and pronounced the necessary private declaration. Those effects are, however, already extended to the other Member States by Art. 44 and 45 PP – with no need for a special recognition regime. The legal effects of the private declarations contained in an authentic instrument set up in one Member State are already 'recognised' by the other Member States based on the duty to apply the law governing the establishment of parenthood under Art. 17 PP. It should also be noted that the formal validity of such private declarations is already favoured by the conflict rules of the Parenthood Proposal, notably by Art. 19 PP. In short, there is no room and need for an additional recognition regime such as that proposed in Art. 35 et seq. PP.

151) It is not surprising that also the Parenthood Proposal is unable to give convincing examples for specific authentic instruments establishing parenthood with binding legal effect. Recital 59 refers to 'a notarial deed of adoption or an administrative decision establishing parenthood following an acknowledgment

of paternity' as examples of such authentic instruments. However, these examples are misguided: none of the Member States still allow private adoptions in notarial deeds. Where the administrative decisions envisaged by the Recitals exist at all in the area of parenthood and can be characterised as civil matters, they would – notwithstanding the *TB* decision (see above para. 146) – have to be characterised as decisions within the meaning of Art. 4(4) PP and, thus, circulate already under Art. 24 et seq. PP. If they do not fulfil those criteria, the Group sees no reason that they should be recognised automatically. Private adoptions – which are also rather problematic because the best interests of the child are not always systematically checked by a court and would often be contrary to public policy (cf. also above para. 103) – are only known to a few third-State legal systems. To such adoptions, however, Art. 35 et seq. PP would not apply because they are restricted to authentic instruments establishing parenthood with binding legal effect in a Member State. The European legislator should not confuse the European citizens and Member State courts and authorities with a recognition regime, which has no plausible scope of application.

SECTION 4
Other provisions

Article 40
Prohibition of review of jurisdiction of the court of origin

The jurisdiction of the court of the Member State of origin establishing parenthood may not be reviewed. The test of public policy referred to in point (a) of Article 31(1) may not be applied to the rules relating to jurisdiction set out in Articles 6 to 9.

Comments

152) Art. 40 PP corresponds to Art. 69 of the Brussels IIb Regulation.

Article 40a
Differences in applicable law

Recognition of a judgment relating to parenthood shall not be refused on the ground that, under the law of the Member State in which recognition is sought, the establishment or termination of parenthood would not be permitted on the basis of the same facts.

Comments

153) In view of the fact that, despite the unification of the conflict rules in Art. 17 et seq. PP, it cannot be ruled out that a Member State must apply other conflict rules on the basis of overriding treaty law (cf. Art. 66 PP), the Group proposes to include a provision such as Art. 40a PP in the tradition of the *acquis communautaire*. It corresponds to Art. 70 of the Brussels IIb Regulation.

154) Art. 40a PP is a special version of Art. 41 PP and it prevents the public policy reservation under Art. 31(a) PP from being interpreted too extensively. While Art. 41 PP prohibits a review of the substance of a court decision given in another Member State, Art. 40a PP prohibits a conflict-of-law review.[46] In the Member State where recognition is sought, it should be irrelevant if the court in the Member State of origin has applied the wrong national law on parenthood from the perspective of the relevant conflict rules in the Member State of recognition. In particular, if there are more liberal provisions in the law on parenthood applicable in the Member State of origin than in the Member State where recognition is sought, circumstances that establish legal parenthood only in the Member State of origin should not prevent recognition merely because, from the perspective of the recognising Member State, another – more restrictive – national law would apply.

155) It should also be irrelevant if the courts in the Member State of origin have applied the correct national law on parenthood under the conflict rules relevant in the Member State of recognition, but from the perspective of the latter the application of this national law should have been denied due to the public policy reservation in the conflict of laws.[47]

---

[46] cf. *Hau*, in Staudinger, 'Bürgerliches Gesetzbuch', 2023, Art. 70 Brussels IIb Regulation para. 3.

[47] cf. *Hau*, in Staudinger, 'Bürgerliches Gesetzbuch', 2023, Art. 70 Brussels IIb Regulation para. 3.

156) However, as the wording shows in comparison with that of Art. 40 PP, in sentence 2, a refusal of recognition due to a violation of the procedural public policy is not completely excluded.[48] In this respect, however, the cases must be exceptional. The prohibition of refusal of recognition expressed in Art. 40a PP may not be circumvented without further ado by reference to public policy.

Article 41
Non-review as to substance

Under no circumstances may a court decision given in another Member State, or an authentic instrument establishing parenthood with binding legal effect in the Member State of origin, be reviewed as to their substance.	Under no circumstances may a court decision *on parenthood* given in another Member State~~, or an authentic instrument establishing parenthood with binding legal effect in the Member State of origin,~~ be reviewed as to their substance.

Comments

157) Art. 41 PP corresponds to Art. 71 of the Brussels IIb Regulation.

158) As the Group proposes to delete Art. 35 to 39 PP (see above para. 143 et seq.), there is no need to refer to authentic instruments establishing parenthood with binding legal effect in Art. 41 PP.

Article 42
Costs

This Chapter shall also apply to the determination of the amount of costs and expenses of proceedings under this Regulation.

Comments

159) Art. 42 PP corresponds to Art. 73 of the Brussels IIb Regulation.

---

[48] On the stricter standard of procedural public policy compared to public policy in the conflict of laws, cf. *Geimer*, 'Internationales Zivilprozessrecht', 8th edition, Otto Schmidt, Cologne, 2020, para. 27 f.

Article 43
Legal aid

1. An applicant who, in the Member State of origin, has benefited from complete or partial legal aid or exemption from costs or expenses shall be entitled, in the proceedings provided for in Article 25(1) and Article 32, to benefit from the most favourable legal aid or the most extensive exemption from costs and expenses provided for by the law of the Member State in which proceedings are brought.

2. An applicant who, in the Member State of origin, has benefited from free proceedings before an administrative authority communicated to the Commission pursuant to Article 71 shall be entitled, in any procedures provided for in Articles 25(1) and 32, to benefit from legal aid in accordance with paragraph 1 of this Article. To that end, that party shall present a statement from the competent authority in the Member State of origin to the effect that he or she fulfils the financial requirements to qualify for the grant of complete or partial legal aid or exemption from costs or expenses.

Comments

160) Art. 43 PP corresponds to Art. 74 of the Brussels IIb Regulation. The Group does not suggest any amendments.

CHAPTER V **AUTHENTIC INSTRUMENTS WITH NO BINDING LEGAL EFFECT**	**AUTHENTIC INSTRUMENTS ~~WITH NO BINDING LEGAL EFFECT~~**
Article 44 **Scope**	
This Chapter shall apply to authentic instruments which have no binding legal effect in the Member State of origin but which have evidentiary effects in that Member State.	This Chapter shall apply to authentic instruments ~~which have no binding legal effect in the Member State of origin but~~ which have evidentiary effects in ~~that~~ *the* Member State *of origin.*
Article 45 **Acceptance of authentic instruments**	
1. An authentic instrument which has no binding legal effect in the Member State of origin shall have the same evidentiary effects in another Member State as it has in the Member State of origin, or the most comparable effects, provided that this is not manifestly contrary to public policy (ordre public) in the Member State where it is presented.	1. An authentic instrument ~~which has no binding legal effect in the Member State of origin~~ shall have the same evidentiary effects in another Member State as it has in the Member State of origin, or the most comparable effects, provided that this is not manifestly contrary to public policy (ordre public) in the Member State where it is presented.
2. The public policy (ordre public) referred to in paragraph 1 shall be applied by the courts and other competent authorities of the Member States in observance of the fundamental rights and principles laid down in the Charter, in particular Article 21 thereof on the right to non-discrimination.	
3. A person wishing to use such an authentic instrument in another Member State may ask the authority that has formally drawn up or registered the authentic instrument in	

the Member State of origin to fill in the form in Annex III describing the evidentiary effects which the authentic instrument produces in the Member State of origin.	
4. The attestation shall contain a statement informing Union citizens and their family members that the attestation does not affect the rights that a child derives from Union law and that, for the exercise of such rights, proof of the parent-child relationship can be presented by any means.	
5. Any challenge relating to the authenticity of such an authentic instrument shall be made before the courts of the Member State of origin and shall be decided upon under the law of that Member State. The authentic instrument challenged shall not produce any evidentiary effect in another Member State as long as the challenge is pending before the competent court.	~~5. Any challenge relating to the authenticity of such an authentic instrument shall be made before the courts of the Member State of origin and shall be decided upon under the law of that Member State. The authentic instrument challenged shall not produce any evidentiary effect in another Member State as long as the challenge is pending before the competent court.~~
6. Any challenge relating to the legal acts or legal relationships recorded in such an authentic instrument shall be made before the courts having jurisdiction under this Regulation and shall be decided upon under the law applicable pursuant to Chapter III. The authentic instrument challenged shall not produce any evidentiary effect in a Member State other than the Member State of origin as regards the matter being challenged as long as the challenge is pending before the competent court.	6. Any challenge relating to the legal acts or legal relationships recorded in such an authentic instrument ~~shall be made before the courts having jurisdiction under this Regulation and~~ shall be decided upon under the law applicable pursuant to Chapter III. The authentic instrument challenged shall not produce any evidentiary effect in a Member State other than the Member State of origin as regards the matter being challenged as long as the challenge is pending ~~before the competent court~~.

7. If the outcome of proceedings in a court of a Member State depends on the determination of an incidental question relating to the legal acts or legal relationships recorded in such an authentic instrument, that court shall have jurisdiction over that question.	7. If the outcome of proceedings in a court *or before another competent authority* of a Member State depends on the determination of an incidental question relating to the legal acts or legal relationships recorded in such an authentic instrument, that court *or other competent authority* shall have jurisdiction over that question.

Comments

161) In most legal systems, parenthood is documented by authentic instruments (in the sense of Art. 4(6) PP), be it in civil status documents or in certified excerpts from civil status registries. These authentic instruments have certain evidentiary effects, for example, they trigger a (rebuttable) legal presumption that certain civil status elements exist,[49] for example, the motherhood or fatherhood of a child (see also Recital 59).

162) Against this background, the Group endorses the approach of the Commission to extend the evidentiary effects of such instruments under the (civil status) law of the Member State of origin (in the sense of Art. 4(7) PP) to the other Member States.

163) However, the proposed Art. 44 and 45 PP mainly copy the provisions of the Succession Regulation, in particular its Art. 59, and need to be adjusted to the civil status particularities of authentic instruments certifying parenthood.

No restriction to authentic instruments which have no binding legal effect in the Member State of origin

164) First, as a minor change, the European legislator should not restrict the acceptance of evidentiary effects based on Art. 45(1) PP to authentic instruments which have no binding legal effect in the Member State of origin. As already discussed, there is no need for a recognition regime for authentic instruments with binding legal effect – for this reason the Group proposes not to adopt Art. 35 to 39 PP (see above para. 143). Furthermore, even if authentic instruments with binding legal effect existed within the European Union, they could also have evidentiary effects regarding certain facts established in the instrument. As

[49] See e.g. Section 54 of the German Civil Status Act.

Art. 35 et seq. PP deal only with the recognition of the instruments' binding legal effects and their contents but not with the evidentiary effects (which cannot be regarded as 'binding legal effects'), there could be gaps and frictions.

165) As a consequence, the Group proposes to apply Chapter V to all authentic instruments on parenthood which have evidentiary effects in the Member State of origin.

No need for a special authenticity procedure in the Member State of origin in the light of the Public Documents Regulation: deletion of Art. 45(5) PP

166) Art. 45(5) PP, which requires a special authenticity procedure in the Member State of origin if the authenticity of the instrument is challenged, was copied from Art. 59(2) of the Succession Regulation.

167) The Group recommends deleting this provision because – unlike in the succession context – there is no need within the European Union for such a special authenticity procedure as far as authentic instruments on parenthood are concerned. This follows mainly from the existence of the Public Documents Regulation (Regulation (EU) 2016/1191 of 6 July 2016 on promoting the free movement of citizens by simplifying the requirements for presenting certain public documents in the European Union [2016] OJ L200/1), which applies to all authentic instruments on parenthood and contains elaborate mechanisms to verify the authenticity of those documents. The application of this existing Regulation is not only reserved in the Parenthood Proposal, cf. Art. 2(2) PP, but the Recitals of the Parenthood Proposal also clarify that the Public Documents Regulation 'includes public documents on birth, parenthood and adoption in its scope', 'deals with the authenticity and the language of such documents' (Recital 9), and should be used:

> as regards the presentation by citizens of certified copies … if they [the authorities] have a reasonable doubt as to the authenticity of a public document on birth, parenthood or adoption or their certified copy presented to them

(Recital 15). This mechanism – and the operation of the Public Documents Regulation – would be thwarted if a future Regulation required an additional special authenticity procedure in the Member State of origin for authentic instruments on parenthood.

Modification of Art. 45(6) PP due to partially misleading wording

168) Furthermore, the Group proposes to modify Art. 45(6) PP, which is misleading in the context of authentic instruments on parenthood.

169) Art. 45(6) PP, which is copied from Art. 59(3) of the Succession Regulation, states in its first sentence that courts competent under Art. 6 et seq. PP shall have jurisdiction for any 'challenge relating to the legal acts or legal relationships recorded in such an authentic instrument', and that those challenges shall be decided upon under the law applicable according to Art. 16 et seq. PP. Whereas the latter is correct, this is not true for the former. Art. 6 et seq. PP only deal with the jurisdiction for 'matters relating to parenthood' and not with appeals against the decisions of civil status officers setting up public documents, for example, under Sections 48 and 49 of the German Civil Status Act. Rather, those procedures are administrative in nature and should not be within the ambit of a future Parenthood Regulation. Otherwise – as civil status officers are not bound by the jurisdiction rules of the Regulation (cf. above para. 22) – courts in one Member State could have to decide on acts of civil status officers of other Member States based on civil status law, hence, on acts of other Member States' authorities based on their public law. Such a jurisdictional regime would not be covered by the legislative competences of the European Union under Art. 81(1) of the Treaty on the Functioning of the European Union, which is restricted to 'judicial cooperation in civil matters' and does not encompass judicial cooperation in administrative matters. Furthermore, such a jurisdictional regime would not be sensible as the courts will not be familiar with the civil status procedures of other Member States.

170) Art. 45(6) PP should be reduced to the clarification that any challenge relating to the legal acts or legal relationships recorded in an authentic instrument on parenthood shall be decided upon under the law determined by Art. 16 et seq. PP. This modification does not prevent any party from starting court proceedings in the Member State competent under Art. 6 et seq. PP to establish or terminate parenthood documented in an authentic instrument or any civil status officer from rebutting a presumption under the law of the Member State of origin, which is extended as an evidentiary effect to the other Member States by Art. 45(1) PP.

Need for a thorough revision of Annex III mentioned in Art. 45(3) PP

171) Art. 45(3) and (4) PP provide that a person wishing to use an authentic instrument on parenthood in another Member State may ask the authority that has formally drawn up or registered the authentic instrument in the Member State of origin, i.e. in most systems civil status officers, to fill in the form provided by Annex III describing the evidentiary effects which the authentic instrument produces in the Member State of origin.

172) Although the Group has not systematically checked Annex III, discussions with German civil status practitioners showed that the form provided in Annex III contains many deficiencies and uncertainties. Civil status officers will

have difficulties using this form in the current shape. The Group does not have the impression that the Commission has consulted the Member State civil status authorities or analysed the different civil status documents currently available in the Member States. For example, not all Member State civil status laws require a reference number for the authentic instrument which shall be mentioned in No. 3.1.3 of the form. Additionally, the terminology in No. 3.2.1 is unclear: what is meant by 'one parent' or by 'the other parent'? Most of the Member States' civil status laws still use other terminology. Moreover, the wording 'provides evidence of … Parenthood' goes too far, as some authentic instruments, for example, instruments on an acknowledgment of parenthood, only give evidence as to the declarations of the parties and not as to the legal relationships, such as the parenthood of the acknowledging person. In addition, it does not appear to be very efficient to oblige the civil status authorities to specify – as No. 5.2 requires – in every form the evidentiary effects of the authentic instrument concerned. The exact scope and content of the evidentiary effects raise complicated questions of national civil status and procedural law. The Group suggests that the European legislator requires the Member States to list the necessary, relevant information online and provide a guide to avoid that authorities, even in the same Member State, fill in the forms differently.

173) Furthermore, the relationship between the form in Annex III and the mechanisms of the Public Documents Regulation and the pertinent conventions of the International Commission on Civil Status, should be clarified; the application of these Conventions is also reserved by the Parenthood Proposal, cf. Art. 66(4) PP. Those instruments provide sufficient tools to standardise the content of civil status documents and to make them easily comprehensible for European citizens and Member State authorities in a cross-border context. Furthermore, they have been much more tested in practice and do not contain comparable deficiencies and uncertainties such as the form in Annex III (see above para. 172). The Group sees no need for another multilingual form. The European legislator should not add more bureaucracy for the European citizens and Member State authorities.

174) As a consequence, the Group strongly urges the European legislator to approach the Member State civil status authorities in order to be able to draft forms which can be used in practice, bearing in mind that the civil status documents, and, hence, also the forms provided in Annex III, will have to be issued by the Member State civil status authorities on a daily basis.

Adjustment of Art. 45(7) PP

175) For the proposed changes in Art. 45(7) PP, see above para. 112 on Art. 24(3) PP.

CHAPTER VI
EUROPEAN CERTIFICATE OF PARENTHOOD

Article 46
Creation of a European Certificate of Parenthood

1. This Regulation creates a European Certificate of Parenthood ('the Certificate') which shall be issued for use in another Member State and shall produce the effects listed in Article 53.

2. The use of the Certificate shall not be mandatory.

3. The Certificate shall not take the place of internal documents used for similar purposes in the Member States. However, once issued for use in another Member State, the Certificate shall also produce the effects listed in Article 53 in the Member State whose authorities issued it in accordance with this Chapter.

Comments

176) Art. 46 PP is intended to introduce a European Certificate of Parenthood (short: 'the Certificate') as a new European legal instrument. The Certificate 'is for use by a child or a legal representative who, in another Member State, needs to invoke the child's parenthood status' (Art. 47 PP). According to Art. 46(2) PP, the use of the Certificate shall not be mandatory. However, if the child decides to make use of the Certificate:

> no authority or person presented with a European Certificate of Parenthood issued in another Member State should be entitled to request that a court decision or an authentic instrument be presented instead of the European Certificate of Parenthood.[50]

---

[50] Recital 78, sentence 3.

The Certificate is apparently modelled on the European Certificate of Succession (Art. 62 et seq. of the Succession Regulation), which has served as a blueprint for the provisions in Chapter VI of the Parenthood Proposal.

177) Art. 46 PP corresponds to Art. 62 of the Succession Regulation.

No need for the creation of a European Certificate of Parenthood

178) The creation of an optional European Certificate of Parenthood is one of the central concerns of the Commission. The Certificate is 'designed specifically to facilitate the recognition of parenthood within the Union'.[51] In particular, the Certificate is intended to 'reduce the administrative burden of the recognition procedures and translation costs for all families'.[52] These are important objectives. On closer examination, however, there are doubts as to whether the Certificate is suitable and necessary to achieve the intended goals. This is not only true against the background that the requirements and effects of the Certificate as set out in the Parenthood Proposal do not yet appear fully developed (cf. the comments on Art. 46 et seq. PP). There is also the fundamental question whether the Certificate in its proposed form has a significant added value compared to the recognition of court decisions and authentic instruments with binding legal effect (Art. 24 et seq. PP)[53] on the one hand, and to the acceptance of authentic instruments with no binding legal effect (Art. 44 and 45 PP) on the other hand.

179) According to the explanatory memorandum to the Parenthood Proposal, the Certificate (as opposed to national certificates of birth or parenthood) shall be issued always through the same procedure, in a uniform standard form and with the same contents and effects throughout the European Union.[54] The greatest weight is likely to be attached to the uniform effects. However, it should be noted that the effects of the Certificate are ultimately limited to the presumption set out in Art. 53(2) PP and the effect according to Art. 53(3) PP. Unlike the European Certificate of Succession, the European Certificate of Parenthood has no bona fide effect. The effects of the European Certificate of Parenthood are, therefore, much weaker than is the case with the European Certificate of Succession.

---

[51] See COM(2022) 695 final, p. 17; cf. also Recital 76.

[52] See COM(2022) 695 final, p. 9.

[53] cf. on the Group's proposal to dispense with the proposed rules on authentic instruments with binding legal effect (Art. 35 to 39 PP) the above remarks under para. 143 et seq.

[54] See COM(2022) 695 final, p. 17; cf. also Recital 80.

180) According to Art. 53(2) PP, the Certificate:

> shall be presumed to demonstrate accurately elements which have been established under the law applicable to the establishment of parenthood. The person mentioned in the Certificate as the child of a particular parent or parents shall be presumed to have the status mentioned in the Certificate.

If Art. 53(2) PP is understood in the same way as the parallel provision in the Succession Regulation, the Certificate establishes a presumption of law and fact (cf. below para. 205 and 199). It is not explicitly stated whether the presumption under Art. 53(2) PP is rebuttable. However, as the provision is closely modelled on Art. 69(2) of the Succession Regulation, it can probably be assumed that the European Certificate of Parenthood (as accepted for the European Certificate of Succession) merely creates a rebuttable presumption (cf. also below para. 206).[55] This means that proof to the contrary is admissible (on the requirements for rebuttal, cf. below para. 206).[56] The presumption under Art. 53(2) PP (and its rebuttability) can be important in different contexts. The cases concerned are, firstly, those in which the child asserts claims or rights, such as when child maintenance is demanded, or a statutory right of inheritance is asserted. The question of the existence of a parent-child relationship arises here as a preliminary question. In such cases, Art. 53(2) PP reverses the burden of proof. It can be assumed that the presumption under Art. 53(2) PP can be rebutted both by proof of deviating facts (e.g. time of birth of the child or sexual intercourse with the mother during the period of conception) and on legal grounds (e.g. invalidity of the marriage of the mother with the presumptive second parent). The most relevant scenarios are likely to be those in which the legal situation demonstrated in the Certificate does not correspond to the legal situation in the Member State of use. This is conceivable, notwithstanding the unified conflict rules in Chapter III, e.g. if the conflict rules for certain preliminary questions (e.g. marriage) differ,[57] or if overriding international conventions apply (see Art. 66(1) PP). In such cases, the Certificate cannot be used as proof of

---

[55] See, on Art. 69(2) of the EU Succession Regulation, *Budzikiewicz*, in Calvo Caravaca/Davì/Mansel, 'The EU Succession Regulation', Cambridge University Press, Cambridge 2016, Art. 69 para. 9 with further references.

[56] See, on Art. 69(2) of the EU Succession Regulation, *Dutta*, in Säcker/Rixecker/Oetker/Limperg, 'Münchener Kommentar zum Bürgerlichen Gesetzbuch', 9th edition, C.H. Beck, Munich 2024, Art. 69 EuErbVO para. 12; *Budzikiewicz*, in Calvo Caravaca/Davì/Mansel, 'The EU Succession Regulation', 2016, Art. 69 para. 9.

[57] cf. Recital 80, sentence 3: 'The evidentiary effects of the European Certificate of Parenthood should not extend to elements which are not governed by this Regulation, such as the civil status of the parents of the child whose parenthood is concerned.'

parenthood. The effects of the Certificate are, therefore, much weaker than those of the recognition of a court decision or an authentic instrument with binding legal effect (cf. Art. 24 et seq. PP).[58] At best, the Certificate is advantageous in comparison to the acceptance of an authentic instrument with no binding legal effect, which only has evidentiary effects (Art. 45 PP). However, the cases in which this advantage pays off are likely to be rare. A party disputing the parenthood documented in an authentic instrument with no binding legal effect (e.g. national certificates of birth or parenthood) will bring forth the same arguments as against a European Certificate of Parenthood with the same content. The differences in the burden of presentation and proof will rarely become manifest.

181) Furthermore, it also seems unclear how far the presumption according to Art. 53(2) PP should extend with regard to the personal scope of the provision. With regard to the European Certificate of Succession, some argue that its effects only arise in disputes between a (presumed) heir and a third party, but not in disputes between the (presumed) heirs themselves.[59] Should a correspondingly narrow understanding also apply to the European Certificate of Parenthood (for which there is some evidence), its scope of application would be considerably reduced. This does not only apply to cases where the question of parenthood is the main question. Even in a dispute where parenthood becomes relevant only as a preliminary question, it would be inappropriate if Art. 53(2) PP restricted the possibility of the person concerned to defend himself or herself by denying his or her parenthood. This applies in particular in cases where the presumptive parent has not been included in the establishment of parenthood (e.g. because parenthood was established by operation of law).

182) Of course, the presumption under Art. 53(2) PP also binds courts and authorities of the Member States. This circumstance may be relevant, for example, when the issuance of identity documents is requested with reference to the European Certificate of Parenthood (e.g. because the acquisition of the nationality of the Member State concerned is based on a *ius sanguinis*). However, it can be assumed that the presumption under Art. 53(2) PP is also rebuttable in this case (by proof of deviating facts and for legal reasons; cf. above para. 180). An authority is thus not required to issue identity documents if the

---

[58] cf. also *Fulchiron*, 'La proposition de règlement européen sur la filiation: coup de maître ou coup d'épée dans l'eau ?', Journal du droit international 2023 (4), 1171–1208, p. 1199 (*'[le certificat] est à mi-chemin entre l'acte d'état civil et la décision de justice ou l'acte authentique ayant un effet juridique contraignant'*).

[59] See *Fornasier*, in Dutta/Weber, 'Internationales Erbrecht', 2nd edition, C.H. Beck, Munich 2021, Art. 69 EuErbVO para. 9.

presumption under Art. 53(2) PP is rebutted. Ultimately, it can be assumed that an authority which is to make a decision for which the parenthood shown in the Certificate is relevant as a preliminary question, will, in principle, check whether the underlying factual and (above all) legal circumstances are correctly stated from its point of view. However, this clearly reduces the intended effects of the Certificate.

183) Art. 53(3) PP clarifies that the European Certificate of Parenthood also has effect for the registration of parenthood in the registers of the Member States. The provision stipulates that the Certificate 'shall constitute a valid document for the recording of parenthood'. A comparable regulation can be found in Art. 69(5) of the Succession Regulation. Based on the interpretation of Art. 69(5) of the Succession Regulation,[60] it can be assumed that the registration authority shall accept the European Certificate of Parenthood as evidence of the status mentioned therein; it cannot require that a court decision or an authentic instrument be presented instead of the Certificate. It should be noted, however, that in the literature on Art. 69(5) of the Succession Regulation, it is disputed whether the authority may refuse registration if there are reasonable doubts as to the accuracy of the content of the European Certificate of Succession.[61] The same question arises with regard to Art. 53(3) PP. Doubts as to the obligation of Member States to record parenthood exist in particular where the certified status conflicts with the law of the Member State concerned (on possible reasons for this, cf. above para. 180). An obligation to record would, in any case, contradict the rebuttability of the presumption under Art. 53(2) PP. Thus, in relation to Art. 53(2) PP, Art. 53(3) PP would only have an independent significance if the registration of parenthood is required for acquiring or establishing rights based on parenthood. However, it is unlikely that this will be relevant in many cases because registration of parenthood is, in general, not constitutive for establishing parental rights (for the effects of recording or failing to record parenthood in a register of a Member State, see also Art. 3(2)(i) PP).

184) Against this background, the question arises whether the European Certificate of Parenthood is needed in addition to the acceptance of authentic instruments with no binding legal effect (and the recognition of court decisions and authentic instruments with binding legal effect). This is all the more true in view of the fact that the Certificate shall be issued in the Member State 'in which parenthood was established' (see Art. 48(1) PP). According to Annex IV No. 3,

---

[60] See *Budzikiewicz*, in Calvo Caravaca/Davì/Mansel, 'The EU Succession Regulation', 2016, Art. 69 para. 18.

[61] See, on this dispute, *Budzikiewicz*, in Calvo Caravaca/Davì/Mansel, 'The EU Succession Regulation', 2016, Art. 69 para. 18; *Fornasier*, in Dutta/Weber, 'Internationales Erbrecht', 2nd edition, 2021, Art. 69 EuErbVO para. 30b.

this phrase designates the Member States in which parenthood was established by a court or another competent authority or in which an authentic instrument was issued with evidentiary effects in the Member State of origin (see also below para. 190). Therefore, before the Certificate is issued, there must always exist a national certificate of birth or parenthood which, according to the Parenthood Proposal, also has to be recognised or accepted in the other Member States (and for which uniform standard forms are provided). Hence, it remains unclear what added value the Certificate provides, apart from the uniform presumption in Art. 53(2) PP, which is however (as was already said) rebuttable.

185) For this reason, the Group rejects the introduction of a European Certificate of Parenthood in the form proposed. Should the European legislator, nonetheless, decide to introduce the Certificate, Art. 46 et seq. PP should be thoroughly revised. The following comments make some suggestions.

Article 47
Purpose of the Certificate

The Certificate is for use by a child or a legal representative who, in another Member State, needs to invoke the child's parenthood status.	The Certificate is for use by a child *or a relative* ~~a legal representative~~ who~~,~~ *needs to prove the parenthood* in another Member State~~, needs to invoke the child's parenthood status~~.

Comments

186) Art. 47 PP corresponds to Art. 63(1) of the Succession Regulation.

187) Art. 47 PP so far only mentions the child or a legal representative as potential users of the European Certificate of Parenthood. The view of the Parenthood Proposal is thus narrowed exclusively to the interests of the child. Other possible users are left out. However, this ignores the fact that not only the child, but also his or her relatives acquire a number of rights from parenthood (cf. Recital 11). For example, the child's parents may have their own interests in the use of the Certificate, e.g. if they claim a right of residence based on parenthood. Similarly, the child's descendants may have an interest in proving their descent from the grandparents, for example, to obtain identity documents or to assert inheritance rights based on parenthood. The Group therefore considers that the circle of users should be extended to include the child's parent(s) as well as other relatives, as far as they have to prove the parenthood in another Member State.

188) Moreover, it is not necessary to mention the legal representative of the child. It is self-evident that minor children are usually represented by their parents or other legal representatives. The need for representation of the child is a matter of (national) substantive family law which falls outside the scope of the Parenthood Proposal.

Article 48
Competence to issue the Certificate

1. The Certificate shall be issued in the Member State in which parenthood was established and whose courts, as defined in Article 4(4), have jurisdiction under Article 6, Article 7 or Article 9.	1. The Certificate shall be issued in the Member State in which parenthood was established and whose courts, as defined in Article 4(4), have jurisdiction *pursuant to Chapter II* ~~under Article 6, Article 7 or Article 9~~.
2. The issuing authority, as communicated to the Commission pursuant to Article 71, of the Member State referred to in paragraph 1 shall be: (a) a court as defined in Article 4(4); or (b) another authority which, under national law, has competence to deal with parenthood matters.	

Comments

189) Art. 48 PP corresponds to Art. 64 of the Succession Regulation.

190) Art. 48(1) PP should be clarified. The wording 'the Member State in which parenthood was established' does not make clear which acts are to be decisive. As stated by the Commission in its Explanatory Memorandum, parenthood 'is typically established by operation of law or by an act of a competent authority, such as a court decision, a decision by an administrative authority or a notarial deed'.[62] However, the wording of Art. 48(1) PP suggests that only the latter

[62] See COM(2022) 695 final, p. 11.

cases should be covered by the provision. Annex IV No. 3 goes even further and also includes cases in which a 'competent authority … issued an authentic instrument with no binding legal effect but with evidentiary effects in the Member State of origin'.[63] This should cover most cases. However, scenarios in which parenthood has been established by mere operation of law (on the basis of the rules determined in accordance with the future Regulation) but no authentic instrument has (yet) been issued are not covered: the establishment of parenthood by operation of law cannot – in a strict sense – be located in a particular Member State. In this case, the question arises whether a Certificate can be issued in any Member State whose courts have jurisdiction pursuant to Chapter II, or whether the issuance of a Certificate has to be declined as long as parenthood is not yet registered. In the former case, the risk of contradictory certificates cannot be ruled out.[64]

191) It is also unclear how cases are to be treated in which the birth of a child is first registered in a foreign country and only then in a Member State (in Germany, e.g. in case of a *Nachbeurkundung*). The question arises whether one can still speak of an 'establishment in a Member State' if only the second registration took place there.

192) Art. 48(1) PP cumulatively requires that the courts of the Member State in which the Certificate is to be issued have jurisdiction under Art. 6, 7 or 9 PP. According to the wording, the courts must have jurisdiction at the time of issuance. This raises the question of whether to deny the issuance of the Certificate in cases where the courts had jurisdiction at the time parenthood was established but not at the time the Certificate was applied for. Such cases should be rare due to the wide jurisdictional rules. However, they cannot be ruled out (e.g. with regard to refugees).

193) The Group recommends extending the reference in Art. 48(1) PP to all jurisdictional provisions in Chapter II. This corresponds to the broad wording in Recital 79. Through this extension, Art. 14 PP in particular would be applicable. This is important in case the application for a Certificate is filed in different Member States.

---

[63] cf. also Art. 49(3)(d) PP.

[64] cf. also *González Beilfuss*, Revue trimestrielle de droit européen 2023 (2), 217–231. On the problem of conflicting European Certificates of Succession, cf. *Dutta*, in 'Münchener Kommentar zum Bürgerlichen Gesetzbuch', 9th edition, 2024, Art. 69 EuErbVO para. 35.

Article 49
Application for a Certificate

1. The Certificate shall be issued upon application by the child ('the applicant') or, where applicable, a legal representative.

1. The Certificate shall be issued upon application by the child *or a relative* ('the applicant') or, where applicable, a legal representative.

2. For the purposes of submitting an application, the applicant may use the form established in Annex IV.

3. The application shall contain the information listed below, to the extent that such information is within the applicant's knowledge and is necessary in order to enable the issuing authority to certify the elements which the applicant wants certified, and shall be accompanied by all relevant documents either in the original or by way of copies which satisfy the conditions necessary to establish their authenticity, without prejudice to Article 50(2):

(a) details concerning the applicant: surname(s) (if applicable, surname(s) at birth), given name(s), sex, date and place of birth, nationality (if known), identification number (if applicable), address;

(b) if applicable, details concerning the legal representative of the applicant: surname(s) (if applicable, surname(s) at birth), given name(s), address and representative capacity;

(c) details concerning each parent: surname(s) (if applicable, surname(s) at birth), given name(s), date and place of birth, nationality, identification number (if applicable), address;

(d) the place and Member State where the parenthood of the child is registered;

(e) the elements on which the applicant founds parenthood, appending the original or a copy of the document(s) establishing parenthood with binding legal effect or providing evidence of the parenthood;

(f) the contact details of the Member State's court that established parenthood, of the competent authority that issued an authentic instrument establishing parenthood with binding legal effect, or of the competent authority that issued an authentic instrument with no binding legal effect in the Member State of origin but with evidentiary effects in that Member State;

(g) a declaration stating that, to the applicant's best knowledge, no dispute is pending relating to the elements to be certified;

(h) any other information which the applicant deems useful for the purposes of the issuance of the Certificate.

Comments

194) Art. 49 PP corresponds to Art. 65 of the Succession Regulation.

195) Art. 49(1) PP should be amended for the reasons stated above in para. 187.

196) If the proposals above in para. 187 concerning the group of persons entitled to file applications are adopted, Art. 49(3) PP would have to be amended accordingly.

Article 50
Examination of the application

1. Upon receipt of the application, the issuing authority shall verify the information and declarations and the documents and other evidence provided by the applicant. It shall carry out the enquiries necessary for that verification of its own motion where this is provided for or authorised by its national law, or shall invite the applicant to provide any further evidence which it deems necessary.

2. Where the applicant has been unable to produce copies of the relevant documents which satisfy the conditions necessary to establish their authenticity, the issuing authority may decide to accept other forms of evidence.

3. Where this is provided for by its national law and subject to the conditions laid down therein, the issuing authority may require that declarations be made on oath or by a statutory declaration in lieu of an oath.

4. For the purposes of this Article, the competent authority of a Member State shall, upon request, provide the issuing authority of another Member State with information held, in particular, in the civil, personal or population registers and other registers recording facts of relevance for the parenthood of the applicant, where that competent authority would be authorised, under national law, to provide another national authority with such information.

4. For the purposes of this Article, the competent authority of a Member State shall, upon request, provide the issuing authority of another Member State with information held, in particular, in the civil, personal or population registers and other registers recording facts of relevance for the parenthood of the ~~applicant~~*child*, where that competent authority would be authorised, under national law, to provide another national authority with such information.

Comments

197) Art. 50 PP is equivalent to Art. 66 of the Succession Regulation. The proposed amendment of Art. 50(4) PP is an adaptation to the changes proposed above in para. 187.

Article 51
Issuance of the Certificate

1. The issuing authority shall issue the Certificate without delay in accordance with the procedure laid down in this Chapter when the elements to be certified have been established under the law applicable to the establishment of parenthood. It shall use the form in Annex V.

The issuing authority shall not issue the Certificate in particular if:

(a) the elements to be certified are being challenged; or

(b) the Certificate would not be in conformity with a court decision covering the same elements.

2. The fee collected for issuing a Certificate shall not be higher than the fee collected for issuing a certificate under national law providing evidence of the parenthood of the applicant.

Comments

198) Art. 51(1) PP is equivalent to Art. 67(1) of the Succession Regulation.

199) Art. 51(1) PP provides that the 'issuing authority shall issue the Certificate … when the elements to be certified have been established under the law applicable to the establishment of parenthood'. The term 'elements' used in Art. 51(1) PP is also found in Art. 67(1) of the Succession Regulation. In relation to that provision, it is discussed whether the term 'elements' includes both factual and legal elements.[65] In particular, the German language version, which uses the term '*Sachverhalt*' in both Art. 51(1) PP and Art. 67(1) of the Succession Regulation, leads to ambiguities. In this context, it would be helpful if the Recitals clarified that the term 'elements' refers to factual as well as legal elements. In addition, the German language version should be adapted.

200) According to Art. 51(1) PP, the issuing authority should only issue the Certificate 'when the elements to be certified have been established under the law applicable to the establishment of parenthood'. This requires the issuing authority to review the parenthood already established in the same Member State by the authority first registering parenthood (which does not have to be identical to the authority issuing the Certificate, cf. Art. 48 PP and Recital 79). Such a review is necessary whenever parenthood has not been established by a court decision (or an authentic instrument with binding legal effect) that is binding for the authority issuing the Certificate. Conversely, if the authority first registering parenthood has only issued an authentic instrument with no binding legal effect, the authority issuing the Certificate is not bound by the legal opinion of the authority first registering parenthood. However, it remains unclear what the consequences are if the authority issuing the Certificate reaches a conclusion different from that of the authority first registering parenthood in that Member State. Should the issuing authority be able to issue a Certificate that conflicts with a previously issued authentic instrument, the consequence would

[65] See *Kreße*, in Calvo Caravaca/Davì/Mansel, 'The EU Succession Regulation', Cambridge University Press, Cambridge 2016, Art. 67 para. 2 with further references.

be that conflicting certificates would be in circulation. The Group suggests that the problem should at least be addressed in the Recitals.

201) The Group points out that the grounds for refusal of issuance in Art. 51(1) PP have led to difficulties of interpretation in the corresponding provision of Art. 67(1) of the Succession Regulation.[66] The related questions should be clarified in the Recitals.

Article 52
Contents of the Certificate

The Certificate shall contain the following information, as applicable:

(a) the name, address and contact details of the Member State's issuing authority;

(b) if different, the name, address and contact details of the Member State's court that established parenthood, of the competent authority that issued an authentic instrument establishing parenthood with binding legal effect, or of the competent authority that issued an authentic instrument with no binding legal effect in the Member State of origin but with evidentiary effects in that Member State;

(c) the reference number of the file;

(d) the date and place of issue;

(e) the place and Member State where the parenthood of the child is registered;

[66] See *Kreße*, in Calvo Caravaca/Davì/Mansel, 'The EU Succession Regulation', 2016, Art. 67 para. 6 et seq.; *Fornasier*, in Dutta/Weber, 'Internationales Erbrecht', 2nd edition 2021, Art. 67 EuErbVO para. 4 et seq.

(f) details concerning the applicant: surname(s) (if applicable, surname(s) at birth), given name(s), sex, date and place of birth, nationality (if known), identification number (if applicable), address;

(g) if applicable, details concerning the legal representative of the applicant: surname(s) (if applicable, surname(s) at birth), given name(s), address and representative capacity;

(h) details concerning each parent: surname(s) (if applicable, surname(s) at birth), given name(s), date and place of birth, nationality, identification number (if applicable), address;

(i) the elements on the basis of which the issuing authority considers itself competent to issue the Certificate;

(j) the law applicable to the establishment of parenthood and the elements on the basis of which that law has been determined;

(k) a statement informing Union citizens and their family members that the Certificate does not affect the rights that a child derives from Union law and that, for the exercise of such rights, proof of the parent-child relationship can be presented by any means;

(l) signature and/or stamp of the issuing authority.

Comments

202) If the proposals above in para. 187 concerning the persons entitled to file applications are adopted, Art. 52 PP would have to be amended accordingly.

Article 53
Effects of the Certificate

1. The Certificate shall produce its effects in all Member States without any special procedure being required.	1. *Subject to Article 55(4), the*~~The~~ Certificate shall produce its effects in all Member States without any special procedure being required.
2. The Certificate shall be presumed to demonstrate accurately elements which have been established under the law applicable to the establishment of parenthood. The person mentioned in the Certificate as the child of a particular parent or parents shall be presumed to have the status mentioned in the Certificate.	2. The Certificate shall be presumed to demonstrate accurately elements which have been established under the law applicable to the establishment of parenthood. The person mentioned in the Certificate as the child of a particular parent or parents shall be presumed to have the status mentioned in the Certificate. *The presumptions in this paragraph are rebuttable.*
3. The Certificate shall constitute a valid document for the recording of parenthood in the relevant register of a Member State, without prejudice to point (i) of Article 3(2).	

Comments

203) Art. 53 PP regulates the effects of the European Certificate of Parenthood. The provision corresponds to Art. 69(1), (2) and (5) of the Succession Regulation.

204) The proposed amendment in Art. 53(1) PP contains a clarification resulting from the proposed addition of a new paragraph 4 in Art. 55 PP (see below para. 211).

205) Art. 53(2) PP provides that the 'Certificate shall be presumed to demonstrate accurately elements which have been established under the law applicable to the establishment of parenthood'. An almost identical wording can be found in Art. 51(1) PP. On the question of how the term 'elements' is to be understood, cf. above para. 199.

206) As already stated (above para. 180), it must be assumed that the presumptions in Art. 53(2) PP are rebuttable. In addition to the conceptual consistency with Art. 69(2) of the Succession Regulation (cf. above para. 180), this is also supported by Recital 80, sentence 2. According to this Recital, the Certificate should have 'evidentiary effects'. However, this suggests that the presumptions according to Art. 53(2) PP should only apply as long as the Certificate is not proven to be incorrect. Consequently, the Certificate does not establish the designated elements in a legally binding manner, but only provides a presumption. The Group therefore proposes to clarify the rebuttability of the presumptions in Art. 53(2) PP in a new sentence 3 of the paragraph. In addition, it should be clarified whether the rebuttal of the presumptions should be based on the *lex fori* or whether a European standard is to be applied. The Group is of the opinion that it would be advisable to introduce a European standard clearly stating that the Certificate is to be considered correct until proven otherwise (i.e. proof to the contrary is required). Such a provision would strengthen the effect of the presumption and create clarity.

207) According to Art. 53(3) PP, the 'Certificate shall constitute a valid document for the recording of parenthood in the relevant register of a Member State'. As already stated (above para. 183), the question arises whether the authorities in the other Member States addressed with the Certificate are forced to record parenthood even if they have reasonable doubts as to the accuracy of the contents of the Certificate. The Group assumes that recording cannot be required if it would conflict with the legal situation in the Member State concerned. Should, however, Art. 53(3) PP be meant to establish an obligation to register parenthood even in such a case, the Group suggests deleting the provision. Regardless, a recording would not bring any advantages for the persons concerned because the presumption under Art. 53(2) PP remains rebuttable.[67]

[67] cf. on Art. 69 of the Succession Regulation, *Dutta*, in 'Münchener Kommentar zum Bürgerlichen Gesetzbuch', 9th edition, 2024, Art. 69 EuErbVO para. 30.

Article 54
Certified copies of the Certificate

1. The issuing authority shall keep the original of the Certificate and shall issue one or more certified copies to the applicant or a legal representative.

2. The issuing authority shall, for the purposes of Articles 55(3) and 57(2), keep a list of persons to whom certified copies have been issued pursuant to paragraph 1.

Comments

208) Art. 54 PP corresponds to Art. 70(1) and (2) of the Succession Regulation. Unlike Art. 70(3) of the Succession Regulation, Art. 54 PP does not limit the period of validity for the copies of the Certificate.[68] The Commission is of the opinion that, with regard to 'the stability of parenthood status in the vast majority of cases', the validity of the copies should not be limited in time.[69] The Group wants to add that it would be quite time-consuming for the child (or his/her parents) to be forced to repeatedly apply for an extension of the validity period or for a new certified copy of the Certificate. It is to be expected that the European Certificate of Parenthood will be required again and again in different contexts. The risk of misuse appears to be manageable. This applies not least with regard to the Group's proposal that in the event of a correction, modification or withdrawal, the Certificate and all certified copies lose their effect (below para. 211) and all copies of the Certificate must be returned (below para. 210). In addition, the effects of the European Certificate of Parenthood are much weaker than those of a European Certificate of Succession (see above para. 179 et seq.).

---

[68] cf. the opinion of the Austrian Bar (*Österreichischer Rechtsanwaltskammertag – ÖRAK*), which proposes introducing a provision on the temporary effect of the Certificate along the lines of the European Certificate of Succession in order to promote acceptance within the EU: www.rechtsanwaelte.at/uploads/tx_wxstellungnahmen/OERAK_Stellungnahme_zur_ElternschaftsVO_online.pdf (last accessed 15 January 2024).

[69] See Recital 81, sentence 3.

Article 55
Rectification, modification or withdrawal of the Certificate

1. The issuing authority shall, at the request of any person demonstrating a legitimate interest or of its own motion, rectify the Certificate in the event of a clerical error.

2. The issuing authority shall, at the request of any person demonstrating a legitimate interest or, where this is possible under national law, of its own motion, modify or withdraw the Certificate where it has been established that the Certificate or individual elements thereof are not accurate.

3. The issuing authority shall inform without delay all persons to whom certified copies of the Certificate have been issued pursuant to Article 54(1) of any rectification, modification or withdrawal thereof.

3. The issuing authority shall inform without delay all persons to whom certified copies of the Certificate have been issued pursuant to Article 54(1) of any rectification, modification or withdrawal thereof, *and order the return of all certified copies of the rectified, modified or withdrawn Certificate.*

4. With the rectification, modification or the withdrawal of the Certificate, the Certificate and all certified copies lose their effect.

Comments

209) Art. 55 PP is equivalent to Art. 71 of the Succession Regulation.

210) The Group proposes that in the event of rectification, modification or withdrawal of the Certificate, all persons to whom certified copies of the Certificate have been issued should be required to return them. By reclaiming the certified copies of a rectified, modified or withdrawn Certificate, misuse is prevented.

211) The Group proposes to clarify in a new paragraph 4 that when the Certificate is rectified, modified or withdrawn, the Certificate and all certified copies should lose their effect.

Article 56
Redress procedures

1. Decisions taken by the issuing authority pursuant to Article 51 may be challenged by the applicant for a Certificate or a legal representative.	1. Decisions taken by the issuing authority pursuant to Article 51 may be challenged by the applicant for a Certificate ~~or a legal representative~~.
Decisions taken by the issuing authority pursuant to Article 55 and point (a) of Article 57(1) may be challenged by any person demonstrating a legitimate interest.	
The challenge shall be lodged before a court in the Member State of the issuing authority in accordance with the law of that Member State.	
2. If, as a result of a challenge as referred to in paragraph 1, it is established that the Certificate issued is not accurate, the competent court shall rectify, modify or withdraw the Certificate or ensure that it is rectified, modified or withdrawn by the issuing authority.	
If, as a result of a challenge as referred to in paragraph 1, it is established that the refusal to issue the Certificate was unjustified, the competent court shall issue the Certificate or ensure that the issuing authority re-assesses the case and makes a fresh decision.	

Comments

212) Art. 56 PP is equivalent to Art. 72 of the Succession Regulation.

213) For the reasons stated above (see para. 188), it is not necessary to mention the legal representative of the applicant.

Article 57
Suspension of the effects of the Certificate

1. The effects of the Certificate may be suspended by:

(a) the issuing authority, at the request of any person demonstrating a legitimate interest, pending a modification or withdrawal of the Certificate pursuant to Article 55; or

(b) the court, at the request of any person entitled to challenge a decision taken by the issuing authority pursuant to Article 56, pending such a challenge.

2. The issuing authority or, as the case may be, the court shall without delay inform all persons to whom certified copies of the Certificate have been issued pursuant to Article 54(1) of any suspension of the effects of the Certificate.

During the suspension of the effects of the Certificate no further certified copies of the Certificate may be issued.

The certified copies of the Certificate already issued have no effect during the suspension of the effects of the Certificate.

Comments

214) Art. 57 PP is equivalent to Art. 73 of the Succession Regulation.

215) The suspension of the effects under Art. 57 PP would be meaningless if the certified copies of the Certificate continued to have effect even though the effects of the underlying Certificate were temporarily suspended. Therefore, it should be clarified that the certified copies of the Certificate have no effect during the suspension of the Certificate's effects.

CHAPTER VII
DIGITAL COMMUNICATION

…

CHAPTER VIII
DELEGATED ACTS

…

CHAPTER IX
GENERAL AND FINAL PROVISIONS

…

Comments

216) In Chapters VII to IX, the Group has only commented on Art. 69 PP.

Article 69
Transitional provisions

1. This Regulation shall apply to legal proceedings instituted and to authentic instruments formally drawn up or registered on or after [date of application of this Regulation].	1. This Regulation shall apply to ~~legal proceedings instituted and to authentic instruments formally drawn up or registered~~ *children born* on or after [date of application of this Regulation]. *For children born prior to [date of application of this Regulation], this Regulation shall apply to legal proceedings instituted and to authentic instruments formally drawn up or registered on or after [date of application of this Regulation].* Chapters III *and* VI *do not apply.*

2. Notwithstanding paragraph 1, where the parenthood was established in conformity with one of the laws designated as applicable under Chapter III in a Member State whose courts had jurisdiction under Chapter II, Member States shall recognise:	~~2. Notwithstanding paragraph 1, where the parenthood was established in conformity with one of the laws designated as applicable under~~ Chapter III ~~in a Member State whose courts had jurisdiction under Chapter II, Member States shall recognise:~~
(a) a court decision establishing parenthood in another Member State in legal proceedings instituted prior to [date of application of this Regulation], and	~~(a)a court decision establishing parenthood in another Member State in legal proceedings instituted prior to [date of application of this Regulation], and~~
(b) an authentic instrument establishing parenthood with binding legal effect in the Member State of origin which was formally drawn up or registered prior to [date of application of this Regulation]	~~(b)an authentic instrument establishing parenthood with binding legal effect in the Member State of origin which was formally drawn up or registered prior to [date of application of this Regulation]~~
Chapter IV shall apply to the court decisions and authentic instruments referred to in this paragraph.	~~Chapter IV shall apply to the court decisions and authentic instruments referred to in this paragraph.~~
3. Notwithstanding paragraph 1, Member States shall accept an authentic instrument which has no binding legal effect in the Member State of origin but which has evidentiary effects in that Member State, provided that this is not manifestly contrary to the public policy (ordre public) of the Member State in which acceptance is sought.	3. Notwithstanding paragraph 1, Member States shall accept an authentic instrument ~~which has no binding legal effect in the Member State of origin but~~ which has evidentiary effects in ~~that~~*the* Member State *of origin*, provided that this is not manifestly contrary to the public policy (ordre public) of the Member State in which acceptance is sought.
Chapter V shall apply to the authentic instruments referred to in this paragraph.	Chapter V shall apply to the authentic instruments referred to in this paragraph.

Comments

217) The transitional provision in Art. 69(1) PP provides that the Regulation shall apply to legal proceedings instituted and authentic instruments drawn up or registered on or after the date of the Regulation's application. By this, the Parenthood Proposal more or less adopts the provision in Art. 100(1) of the Brussels IIb Regulation. In Art. 69(2) PP, the intertemporal scope of application is further extended to court decisions in legal proceedings instituted and authentic instruments with binding legal effect, which were formally drawn up or registered prior to the reference date, provided the parenthood was established in conformity with one of the laws designated as applicable under Chapter III in a Member State whose courts had jurisdiction under Chapter II. In addition, the Regulation is intended to apply to authentic instruments which have no binding legal effect in the Member State of origin but which have evidentiary value in that Member State, Art. 69(3) PP.

General rule: clarifying Art. 69(1) PP

218) Art. 69(1) PP only lists legal proceedings and authentic instruments formally drawn up or registered. The European Certificate of Parenthood (Art. 46 et seq. PP) is not mentioned. However, the Parenthood Proposal explicitly distinguishes between authentic instruments (as defined in Art. 4(6) PP) and the European Certificate of Parenthood (cf. e.g. Art. 4(7) PP). Therefore, a wording should be chosen in Art. 69 PP that clearly includes the European Certificate of Parenthood.

219) Art. 69(1) PP does not make any restrictions regarding the date of birth of the child (as defined in Art. 4(2) PP). This means that according to Art. 69(1) PP, the Parenthood Proposal, including the rules on private international law (Chapter III), would also apply to children born before the date of application, provided that the connecting factors mentioned in Art. 69(1) PP occurred on or after this date. However, Art. 69(1) PP leaves open whether, in cases where the child was born before the reference date, the conflict rules of Chapter III should apply retroactively from the date of birth of the child or whether there would be a change of the applicable law on the date of application of the Parenthood Proposal. This question would have to be regulated in the transitional provisions.

220) However, applying the unified conflict rules to children born before the date of application of the Parenthood Proposal poses considerable problems, regardless of whether a change of the applicable law should occur *ex nunc* or *ex tunc*. In both cases, there may be frictions that would have to be resolved by way of adjustment. The problem is aggravated by the fact that, depending on where the legal proceedings are instituted or the authentic instruments are

drawn up or registered on or after the date of application of the Parenthood Proposal, different conflict rules would apply for the period up to the reference date. Thus, depending on the forum, different substantive outcomes may result. The uncertainties involved are problematic for the status of parenthood, which is particularly dependent on legal certainty. They should be avoided as much as possible. The Group, therefore, proposes to apply the conflict rules in Chapter III only to children born on or after the date of application of the Parenthood Proposal.

221) A corresponding restriction should be provided regarding the issuance of the European Certificate of Parenthood. The introduction of the Certificate is justified, not least because the Parenthood Proposal provides for unified conflict rules (cf. Recitals 31 and 80). However, it follows that the Certificate should be issued only if the applicable law was determined by applying the provisions of the future Regulation (see also Art. 51(1) PP). Accordingly, consistent with the Group's proposal for intertemporal applicability of Chapter III, Chapter VI would only apply to children born on or after the date of application of the Regulation (see above para. 220).

222) Apart from this, there is no objection to also apply the provisions of the future Regulation to those children born before the date of application. According to the Group's proposal, this would have the effect that the unified rules on jurisdiction and recognition would apply, but not the conflict rules in Chapter III of the Parenthood Proposal. Problems do not result from this. A comparable situation existed, for example, in divorce law for the period in which the Brussels II Regulation (Council Regulation (EC) 1347/2000 of 29 May 2000 on jurisdiction and the recognition and enforcement of judgments in matrimonial matters and in matters of parental responsibility for children of both spouses [2000] OJ L160/19) or the Brussels IIa Regulation applied, but not the Rome III Regulation, or in maintenance law for the period in which the Brussels I Regulation (Council Regulation (EC) 44/2001 of 22 December 2000 on jurisdiction and the recognition and enforcement of judgments in civil and commercial matters [2001] OJ L12/1) or the Brussels Ia Regulation applied, but not Art. 15 of the Maintenance Regulation in connection with the Hague Maintenance Protocol.

Deletion of Art. 69(2) PP

223) The Group proposes to delete Art. 69(2)(a) PP. With this provision, the Commission apparently intends to make it easier for the persons concerned to prove parenthood even if the legal proceedings in question were instituted before the date of application of the future Regulation. However, the requirements set out in the introductory sentence of Art. 69(2) PP are likely

to cause considerable difficulties in practice. The verification of whether 'the parenthood was established in conformity with one of the laws designated as applicable under Chapter III in a Member State whose courts had jurisdiction under Chapter II' would ultimately have to be made in the State where the court decision was made. For this purpose, a procedure would have to be introduced to ensure the correctness of the verification. The question is whether the effort involved outweighs the benefits of facilitating recognition. This is especially true in light of the fact that verifying 'conformity' need not be easy at all. It is already unclear what is meant by the phrase 'in conformity with one of the laws designated as applicable under Chapter III'. Should the court decision have been made based on one of the laws designated as applicable under Chapter III,[70] or is a corresponding substantive result sufficient, even if it was found based on a law that is not declared applicable under Chapter III? In any case, a legal review would be required. The effort involved speaks against the provision in Art. 69(2)(a) PP.

224) In the Group's view, Art. 69(2)(b) PP can also be deleted. As the Group proposes to delete Art. 35 to 39 PP (see above para. 143 et seq.), the provision in Art. 69(2)(b) PP would be superfluous.

Amendment to Art. 69(3) PP

225) The proposed amendment of Art. 69(3) PP is for clarification purposes only; the wording is an adaptation to the proposals under above para. 143 et seq.

[70] cf. also *González Beilfuss*, Revue trimestrielle de droit européen 2023 (2), 217-231, who points out that due to the innovative conflict rules in Chapter III it is not very likely that the court decision has been made based on one of the laws designated as applicable there.

www.ingramcontent.com/pod-product-compliance
Ingram Content Group UK Ltd.
Pitfield, Milton Keynes, MK11 3LW, UK
UKHW050230160926
8657IPUK00007B/174

9 781839 705137